DIOGE

CW01467965

A quarterly publication of

THE INTERNATIONAL COUNCIL FOR PHILOSOPHY AND HUMANISTIC STUDIES

The English language edition is
sponsored, from issue 153 on, by the
American Council of Learned Societies, New York

Berghahn Books
Providence / Oxford

DIOGENES

Editor: **Jean d'Ormesson**
Deputy Editor: **Paola Costa**

The English language edition of *Diogenes* is published and distributed by

Berghahn Books
165 Taber Avenue, Providence, RI 02906-3329, USA
Tel: (401) 861-9330   Fax (401) 521-0046

Bush House, Merewood Avenue, Oxford OX3 8EF, UK
Tel: (0865) 742 224   Fax (0865) 744 978

to whom all requests concerning subscriptions and information should be addressed. Editorial matters will continue to be handled by the Editor's office in France (*Diogène* – CIPSH, Unesco House, 1 rue Miollis, 75015 Paris).

Each annual volume is published in four issues, including index
Annual Subscriptions
Institutions: US$120.00 / £80.00; Individuals: US$40.00 / £24.00
Agencies: 5% discount
For airmail delivery outside the U.S. add US$20.00 / £11.00

To order, by mail: Carfax Publishing Company, P.O. Box 25, Abingdon, Oxfordshire OX14 3UE, UK or to Carfax Publishing Company, P.O. Box 2025, Dunnellon, Florida 34430-2025, USA

By fax: +44 (0) 235 553559 or to +1-904-489-6996

By telephone: +44 (0) 235 521154 (worldwide, 24 hours, 7 days/week).

Parallel editions published simultaneously:
Arabic edition: National Centre for Unesco Publications, 1 Talaat Harb Street, Tahrir Square, Cairo, Egypt;
French Edition: Gallimard, 5 rue Sébastien Bottin, 75007 Paris;
Spanish edition: Universidad Nacional Autónoma de México, 3er circuito de la Investigación en Humanidades, Dr. Mario de la Cueva, Zona cultural, C.U., c.p. 04510, Mexico, D.F.

The articles published in *Diogenes* express freely the most diverse opinions, for which neither the Editors nor the Publishers can in any way be held responsible.

The journal is not responsible for manuscripts sent to the Editorial Office, nor can it return them unless they are accompanied by International Reply Coupons. Manuscripts are held for one year in the Editorial Office at the disposal of their authors.

Printed in the United States by
Western Newspaper Publishing Co., Indianapolis

ISSN: 0392-1921

DIOGENES

Number 168

Contents

The Social Responsibility of the Historian

Historical Practice and Responsibility

François Bédarida

We are frequently asking ourselves today about the role of the historian in a rapidly changing world. Some expect the past provide them with an explanation or a justification of the present. Others search in history for the basic roots of identity or even for keys to the future. More than ever we are being faced with what Lucien Febvre perceived to be the social function of the historian: "to organize the past as a function of the present." From this arises a responsibility toward society, as the knowledge that is being produced gains its authenticity through being stamped as officially "scientific." Faced with the expectations of society and the attention of the public, the historian has been called upon to disentangle events and to furnish a guiding thread, frequently by blending his role as a critic with a civic and an ethical one. Even when we are not dealing with the attempt to set up the historian, through an appeal to his great expertise, as the licensed sage in town, it must be stressed that assuming the rostrum in response to the questions of the time is-provided that the rules of the discipline are strictly adhered to-perfectly legitimate in that it provides history with signifiant depth.

For all that, some of the great names of historical writing testify to the manifold ways in which historians have intervened in the public space-from de Tocqueville to Palacky, from Croce to Marc Bloch, not to mention Mommsen of whom it might be said that for him the writing of history was merely the continuation of politics by other means! True, we can assert, as Ranke did in his 1836 inaugural lecture, that the study of history and the advance of knowledge, instead of improving the conduct of human affairs, has had negative as well as positive effects. But in reality, history primarily produces questions rather than answers.

Today these questions reinforce all the more the notion that our age is marked by the disintegration of certainties and the collapse of ideologies and that to the crisis of the philosophies of history must be added an explosion of historical knowledge in the wake of an extension of the historian's territory into new fields until now unexplored. However well the historian may be attuned to the world around him, he treads a narrow path between the two contradictory missions that he has been asked to fulfill. On the one hand, he must dissociate himself from those myths that exist in the common mind and from the deformations of collective memory so that he can juxtapose them with a demystifying discourse that is both supported by evidence and rational. On the other hand, as a person who builds and diffuses knowledge he must contribute to the shaping of the historical conscience and the memory of his contemporaries. To put it differently, his being a social actor is inseparable from his being a researcher.

This is why the public frequently calls on him to be an arbiter and authority, recognizing in him his position as a mediator between past and present. In this respect we need merely look at the great historiographical controversies involving large national stakes that have recently taken place in Germany (the clash known as *Historikerstreit*, with its scholarly, political, and moral implications), in France (the case of the 200th anniversary of the Revolution or the current debate on Vichy), or in Italy (where the question of the nature of fascism and its place in the country's history as well as its present resurgence remains a burning issue).

However, if history-as Huizinga has maintained-is a means for society to gain an understanding of what it represents-in its texture as well as its movement-it is still necessary for historiographical construction to respect two basic criteria if we want to avoid its instrumentalization in the nebulous realm of mythologies and propaganda. First, a coherent and explicative relationship between the sources and the referential reality whose indices are the mark; and second, a knowledge gained according to a controlled scientific method and appropriated to its object by following a logic of intelligibility and communication.

It is for these reasons that the responsibility exercised by the historian in his own proper sphere is based on two conditions.

There is first of all independence, be it political or intellectual, social or financial; this is the exigency of liberty. Second, there is the scrupulous and meticulous respect of the canons of the discipline; this is the exigency of truthfulness.

With respect to liberty, the connections between history and power are more complex than they appear at first glance-and not just because next to the power of the state we must also reckon with that of the market, of institutions, and of fashions. True, at all times the political powers have tried to either control or to influence historical writing. But in an inverted sense the historian himself possesses a formidable authority, i.e., that of shaping and legitimizing today's historical consciousness and tomorrow's memory. We all know Chateaubriand's immortal and invigorating warning in his diatribe against Napoleon's despotism:

> When, in the silence of degradation one merely chooses to retain the chains of slavery and the voice of the informer; when everything trembles in the face of the tyrant, and when it is as dangerous to gain his favors as it is to incur his disgrace, the historian appears on the scene, mandated by the vengeance of the people. It did not help Nero to be successful; Tacitus had already emerged under the empire ...

Where can we find a finer demonstration of the historian's cathartic role? But was Chateaubriand, who himself was subjected to imperial wrath, correct in adding: "If the historian's role is a good one, it is often dangerous"; he must have "an intrepid character" and be "prepared for the worst"? Let us remember that the liberal de Toqueville, speaking in 1852 a few months after Napoleon's coup d'état of 2 December during his annual address before the Academy of Moral and Political Sciences, thought it prudent to suppress a damning reference to the brutal closure of this institution by Napoleon I. As to the twentieth century, it too provides many examples of bent backs and timid spirits. In short, the independence of the historian is a *sine qua non* of his being able to pursue his profession and this freedom must extend to both his ability to communicate and to produce knowledge.

At the same time, to the extent that historical understanding is, in Carlo Ginzburg's words, always an understanding that is "indirect, indicated, and conjectural," it lends itself, consciously or unconsciously, to the whole gamut of distortions, if not to breaches of the truth. Let us not speak here of the most flagrant falsifications in the manner of the so-called "revisionists" who deny the genocide of the Jews or of Stalinist specialists in the rewriting of the past (including the top echelon of government, even after a recent biography of Beria revealed that it was he who, in a book entitled *On the History of the Bolshevik Organization in the Transcaucasus*, inaugurated the shift of Soviet historiography into the realm of fiction). For all this, the manipulation of history is an art that has existed at all times. Voltaire, in casting doubt on a history "completely permeated by fables," mocked the absurd stories that were called "history" in Herodotus, Sueton, Tacitus as well as their successors in the Christian era (to mention only Gregory of Tours, "our Herodotus"). In the modern period, the abuse of evidence proliferated, starting with Augustin Thierry's ingenious admission that he was looking in historic narratives for arguments that supported his convictions; or with Treitschke's view that history can be used as a weapon for achieving a political objective, or the I.R.A. radical's statement after an assassination: "History is on our side." Yet the range is very wide between the poison of intellectual deception and the more or less arbitrary and fallacious reconstructions of the past.

It also happens that once every so often a historiographical debate hinges on suspicion if not intentionality. Thus the hypotheses that Fritz Fischer presented in his famous book of 1961 on the origins of World War I were denounced by a well-regarded historian like Gerhard Ritter as being politically dangerous for the historical consciousness of German youth. In a more subtle way and in the name of "critical history," Michael Stürmer has more recently exhorted German historians, working in a society haunted by the memory of its culpability, to anchor patriotism in a positive view of national history by way of developing a sense of identity with the past and of building a consensus with regard to values that overcome political divisions. As he put it, "in the land without history, the future is controlled by those who determine the content of memory, who coin the concepts and interpret the past." Still, if one scrutinizes more closely such an apparently laudable aim, does one not also discern its actual ambiguities and its potential for drifting off into treacherous waters?

4

It is for this reason that it is better to return to the rules of historical practice, to proven rules that lay down both the regulatory and the structuring role of historical knowledge. As Michel de Certeau has so well demonstrated, history, while being a discourse that uses narrative figures, is defined by a scholarly practice based on a "set of rules that allow the 'control' of procedures that are commensurate with the production of the defined object." These rules are those of the critical method first developed in the seventeenth century and later reformulated in the nineteenth. The procedures consist of working out the sequences between the divergent components of the object of study, following the collection, dissection, and critique of the body of available documents. Ultimately this object, whatever its character, invariably is left for the historian to construct. In this sense, historical practice is a scientific one, composed of elements that are falsifiable and controllable, even if it is dependent on the social locus in which it takes place; for it is a function of this locus within society and of this milieu of study that the problematic is being defined, that the stakes are being circumscribed, and the interpretations constructed.

Thus, without minimizing in the slightest the subjective dimension in the work of the historian-it is understandably important to reaffirm, tirelessly, that history must be as objective as possible, even knowing that such an objectivity is never truly attainable, rather than be led astray in the meanderings of post modernist deconstructions. We must choose between scholarship and fiction. What responsibility would remain for the historian if history were merely representation and discourse, as Nietzsche asserted; if there were no truth, but only interpretations? In a universe from which the fixity of the past is banished in favor of an "unassailable relativism" and where history rejoins literature, on what foundations could a future be prepared? In the name of an extreme historicism, post modernism in reality removes all interest in historical research unless it is admired as a brilliant rhetorical exercise. Such skepticism-one might even say nihilism-leads purely and simply to a negation of knowledge, as the latter finds itself reduced to a contingent and arbitrary discourse, an illusion even.

It is from this point that we come back to the need for truthfulness that the historian, instead of minimizing, must proclaim very clearly to be his lode-star. It is a star that is distant, transient, occasionally veiled by clouds, but without it, what could the notion of responsibility be based on? It is true that at this level one enters the realm of values and that a connection between history and ethics is established. But can ethics and responsibility be separated by a watertight partition? Let us moreover note the changes of the *Zeitgeist*. After the radical critique of the 1960s, which destroyed the certainties, buried the utopias and disassembled the beliefs, one has since the 1980s witnessed a return to the values of humanism, morals, and meaning. To be sure, historians have their part in that recasting of intellectual life. They must continue to confront the imperatives of the present.

History and Rhetoric

Paul Ricœur

An inquiry into the rhetorical aspects of history may seem paradoxical, given that historical discourse is not typically included
among those types which, since Aristotle, have been understood
to be governed by rhetoric; these types being the deliberative
council, the tribunal and the commemorative assembly. It was to
these specific audiences that the three kinds of discourse—the
deliberative, judiciary, and panegyric—were addressed. However,
are the boundaries of the historian's audience sufficiently delin-
eated in order to allow us to identify it as a specific addressee?
This first objection, which regards the very legitimacy of the subject of these remarks, can be met by noting a common trait that
links history to the above-mentioned three types of discourse; that
is, competition between opposed discourses requiring a choice. In
each case the aim is to structure a debate that calls for a clear-cut
decision. Yet a major problem of the discipline of history is that it
allows both for widely varying descriptions of the same series of
events, and sanctions the use of a variety of equally acceptable
rules or preferences for interpreting a given slice of the past.

This initial remark leads us to the following inquiry: which
aspects or elements of rhetoric contribute to the formulation of
judgments by the scholarly or general public in regard to works
that the historical profession itself considers worthy of being
included in the universe of historical discourse?

Here, although they may appear to have little in common, two
major accomplishments of rhetoric need to be considered together
—accomplishments which, from the time of Ciceron and Quintilien
down to the latest chairs of rhetoric, have been part of a unique conceptual constellation. Rhetoric, in the first instance, can be characterized by its preference for a type of *argument* that lies somewhere

between the constraints of the necessary and the arbitrariness of the sophistic, between proof and sophistry. This is the probable argument, the theory of which Aristotle outlined in his *Dialectic*, defining rhetoric as the "antistrophe" or counterpart of dialectic. It is precisely in the three typical situations mentioned above that rhetoric applies the logic of the probable, in the form of the art of persuasion; this latter, like the probable argument itself, oscillates between an art of convincing that appeals to reason, and an art of pleasing, even of seduction, that appeals to the passions of the audience. However, driven by its primary aim of influencing an audience, rhetoric did not limit itself to applying the logic of the probable to a theory of argumentation. It developed a second pole, a theory of figures, of turns of phrase or tropes which, since Ramus and Vico, has been based on four essential tropes: metaphor, metonymy, synecdoche, and irony. This component of rhetoric, which became autonomous, manifests the same qualities of ambiguity and instability whether identified as the seat of linguistic creativity, as is the case according to Vico (and therefore the poetic source of all argumentative discourse), or simply an arsenal of ornaments better suited to please than convince. All the major treatises on rhetoric assume that these two groups—argumentation and tropology—are in reality disjoined members of a relatively unified rhetorical field. Discourse here is defined as an activity leading from *inventio* to *memoria* and *pronunciatio*, and includes *dispositio* and *elocutio*. According to the classic formula, a treatise of argumentation covers the heart of *dispositio*, and a treatise on tropes the heart of *elocutio*. In this way the two *membra disjecta* of rhetoric take their place within a living organism.

In what way does this polarization of rhetoric—pulled in turn between argumentation and tropology, or reconstructed in a chain of operations to form a living whole—concern what some historians have called "historical activity?" (*"l'operation historique"*). It concerns it to the extent that this activity can be described as a progression whose three phases are *documentary research, explanation,* and *writing,* this last phase being particularly emphasized in historiographic utterance. If we begin by noting a kinship—at the very least a superficial one—between the rhetoricians' *inventio* and documentary research, between *dispositio* and the stage of explanation, and finally between *elocutio* and the writing of history, we can then

8

reasonably inquire into the existence of ties between oratorical and historical activity that are closer than mere exterior kinship. From the point of view of historical study this investigation is necessitated by the current difficulty in establishing a connection between the epistemological approach to history, which emphasizes the degree of scientific validity of historical explanation, and the approach that might best be called literary, which tends to focus on the manner in which history is written. To call this a difficulty is to understate the nature of the problem. In truth we are currently witnessing a progressive divorce between theories centered on the question of proof in history, and those theories oriented toward investigations of the ways in which historical narrative uses style in order to present the past by giving an illusion of a real presence. In some sense this divorce reproduces the one that divides the field of rhetoric between those who, like Charles Perelman, hold that a theory of argumentation is the only true issue for rhetoric, and those others, like the Russian Formalists and their French imitators, who have restored the tropological approach to a place of honor. Should not the task of a critical philosophy of history be to argue against this dismemberment? Should it not instead strive to harmonize *research and writing* within a unified framework of historical activity, in the same way that argumentation and tropology were once harmonized in the progression joining *inventio, dispositio, elocutio, memoria, pronunciatio* within a public discourse destined for deliberative bodies of political, judiciary, or sumptuary character?

This being my hypothesis, I will now take up the three successive stages of historical activity: documentary research, explanation, and writing. While doing so I will inquire into the manner in which borrowings from the rhetoric of argumentation—including both the stages of *inventio* and *dispositio* of Ancient rhetoric, and the borrowings from the rhetoric of tropes, which constitutes the core of the *elocutio*—contribute to a better understanding of historical activity.

Documentary Research and *inventio*

Even the initial phase of documentary research, which is the gathering of "sources," amply demonstrates that historical activ-

ity involves a rhetorical dimension comparable to the *inventio*.
Equally, the *inventio* of the Ancients was not merely a search for
arguments but of proofs capable of establishing both the topic
and content of the discourse: material or factual proofs, artificial
proofs, that is to say derived from art and that the treatises have
also called "occasions" *(lieux)*. However, in historical research too
the sources are essentially composed of accounts of witness
whose credibility has to be weighed. Of course, unlike public discourse whose aim is to please rather than convince, the gathering
of sources involves a critical approach that already anticipates the
argumentative character of history. The source here takes on a
documentary value, and the verification of an historical fact
through a convergence of sources can lay claim to being documentary evidence. Yet this opposition of *inventio* and documentary criticism is not absolute. Any gathering of sources is guided
by a working hypothesis that is already dependent on the
explanatory phase. This orientation of the inquiry has two
aspects, both of which invite comparison with the *inventio*. On the
one hand, spurred by its investigative question, the search for
documents takes on an unlimited scope; for contemporary historians anything can become a document; market price-lists, parish
records, wills, lists of statistical data, graphs, etc. Anything that
an historian can *question* *(interroger)* becomes a document, since
information about the past can be found there. In this sense modern historical research can be characterized by what Paul Veyne
calls "the lengthening of the questionnaire"; yet it is the explanatory hypothesis itself that determines this lengthening. Thus, on
the other hand, the widening of potential documentary sources
has as its counterpart a strict selection process regarding which of
the remaining parts can be promoted to the rank of document. In
this sense nothing in itself is a document, even if all residue of the
past is a potential trace. From this point of view, research and
explanation now become complementary activities, as if *inventio*
and *compositio* were entangled in an all-inclusive notion of historical research. To this observation it will later be necessary to add
that an explanatory hypothesis is also ultimately a compositional
structure, and that therefore explanation and writing—relatives
of *compositio* and *elocutio*—conjointly preside over *inventio*, which

in historical study takes the form of source criticism and the problematics of documentary evidence. In this way the argumentative character of historical activity is already anticipated in the documentary phase.

Historical explanation and *dispositio*

This argumentative character comes most clearly to the fore on the level of. explanation. It is my assertion that the critique to which the nomological model of Carl G. Hempel (commonly designated the "covering law model" or CLM) has been subjected over the last few decades amounts to an acknowledgment of an epistemological status for history; an acknowledgement based on probable logic and thus also of rhetoric considered as the antistrophe of dialectic in the Aristotelian sense of the term. What was considered as a "weakening" of the CLM was in fact an evolutionary process leading from necessary logic to probable logic; it was not, as has been too easily asserted, the removal of history's scientific status and subsequent re-classification as an art. Although historical proof does not go beyond the verification of isolated facts based on a convergence of testimony (that is to say does not go beyond what is called documentary evidence), history nevertheless persists in arguing in favor of an explanation, that is to say, a sequence of facts that are opposed to another plausible sequence.

Let us now, as regards argumentation, take a look at several of the arguments advanced by some theoreticians laying claim to the heritage of analytic philosophy: Arthur Danto, W.B. Gallie, Charles Frankel, William Dray, and above all Louis O. Mink. It must first be conceded that the historian him or herself does not establish the laws that figure in the major premise of Hempel's deduction but rather is limited to using these laws, which in some sense is reminiscent of the theory of "occasions" of ancient rhetoric. Moreover, it has been observed that historians make use of a very heterogeneous set of rules regarding levels of universality, that the range of acceptable answers to the question of *why* in history is very broad, and that the idea of cause in history has a widely-accepted polysemy. Another observation: the "weighing" of the degrees of importance of such or such presumed cause depends on a logic of "pretensions," "refutations," and "guarantees" that Stephen E. Toulmin thoroughly analyses in a study appropriately entitled *The Uses of Argument*. In this book Toulmin emphasizes, as we did at the outset of this article, how much argument depends on competition between rival interpretations among which a choice must be made.

There exist numerous other connecting frameworks, irreducible to the CLM schema, that are nevertheless endowed with an effective explanatory power. In this sense the explanations found in works of history constitute a logically disparate assemblage, and the term "because" implies no logically predetermined structure. For the purposes of this article I will limit myself to several examples of sequence where the idea of law is succinctly expressed. We will begin with the imputation of singular causality, independently analyzed by Max Weber, Raymond Aron and William Dray: here the test of a candidate's claim to occupying the place of determinant cause will be based on imagining its absence and by comparing the consequences of this absence with the best attested probable course of events. Another explanatory framework would be an explanation based on reasons (the "rational" explanation according to Dray); and the argument would consist of a reconstruction of the agent's calculation, taking into account the considerations that convinced the agent that he should act as he did. A more refined approach to explanation, based on the concept of intervention, has been proposed by George Henrik Von Wright in his book *Explanation and Understanding*. Intervention, from the point of view of the agent, is the attempt to carry out a practicable action that will coincide with the initial stage of a system whose determining closure is caused by setting the system in motion. On the basis of this connection between an intuitively understood "I can" and a causal nexus dependent on an explanatory system, it becomes possible to conjoin, using a mixed model on the level of history, a teleological explanation bearing on intentions with a causal explanation bearing on states of a system. The title of Von Wright's work is well chosen: it can be said that his mixed model belongs to a treatise on argumentation in which argument implies reconciling explanation and understanding.

Having completed this rapid survey of a variety of frameworks used to establish historical connection, we can now return to our initial question: to what extent can the various ways of arguing be identified with the *dispositio* of traditional rhetoric? The answer to this question will be a cautiously positive one, with the necessary caveats enumerated below. What allows us to use the term *compositio* for the various forms of sequencing proposed by historians who strive to explain facts uncovered by source criticism is the narrative form that historical explanation—even the forms of historical explanation closest to the nomological model—inevitably takes on. Let us analyze, for example, the case of an accidental explosion of a gas tank: one could well detail a series of laws relating to the resistance of materials, to overheating, etc.: yet the crucial point is that the case be recounted *seratim*, by reconstituting each phase of the accident, which then takes on the form of a story. As a general rule it must be conceded that even a story as disparate as possible from the kind that the *Annales* school called "event-oriented history" (*histoire événmentielle*), that is to say the narration of brief events that punctuate political, diplomatic and military history in particular, would still require a narrative form in order to account for the changes that a nation, a State, a social class—in short any historical entity—goes through, taking it from an initial to a terminal phase by way of a series of transformations. Among the latter must be included even those events that have been reduced to "an observed discontinuity in a model."[1] From this standpoint the narrative form is not merely superimposed on the explanation (in one of the senses enumerated above) but is consubstantial with it, as the inevitable obedience to chronology bears witness. What narratology as the science of story has shown is that the story (*récit*), even in its popular and folklore forms, has an inherent explanatory value. It does not limit itself to saying: the King died, the Queen died. It says: the King died, then the Queen died of grief. A "because" has sneaked in between the two events, testifying to the fact that even the most insubstantial story contains a passage from "this and then that" to "this because of that." It is the story's inherent explanatory potential that history raises to a higher critical level, and in so doing makes the narrative connection itself a mode of argument.

13

This explanatory capability has been particularly stressed by the English language "narrative" school of history. Of the authors mentioned above I will here only recall Louis O. Mink: besides the fact that his work most fully embodies the thesis of the explanatory value of narrative form, it is also the first step in the transition from the question of explanation to the question of writing which I will take up later. Let us for the moment limit our discussion to the relationship between narrativity and explanation. Mink proposes a concept of narrative explanation that is strongly reminiscent of the idea of *dispositio* of traditional rhetoric. What he calls understanding is relevant beyond the field of history and can indeed be applied to any judgmental activity whose aim is to "hold together," in a single image, a medley of experiences undergone *seriatim*. Story is only one of its modes, that is to say the configuring mode, linking events, episodes and periods in a single sequence or within a complex whole invested with its own identity. Through this concept Mink rediscovers the idea of "colligation," which he learned from his teacher Walsh; and with Mink the story's very form becomes a cognitive tool.

Does this mean that *dispositio* and *historical understanding* are completely synonymous? The key here is not that story is but a form of understanding and therefore one form of *compositio* among others. What is crucial is what I will cautiously call the filiation between history as a social science and the traditional story. However, at the very same time that the extreme complexity of the story was being emphasized by the narratologists, the opponents of historical narrative, in particular the French *Annales* school, continued to underestimate the organizational resources of the story. Happily, this was not the case with all French historians. Paul Veyne, for instance, in *How History is Written*[2], made use of the notion of plot or intrigue, which comes from Aristotle's *Poetics*, as the driving force of historical knowledge: a plot, he wrote, is "a very human and very 'unscientific' mixture of material causes, of ends and accidents." For as long as this disparate combination can be recognized as such there is a plot. From this point of view an event is not only, as has been claimed, a noticeable discontinuity in a structure; rather, in order to invest it with meaning, the event must first be told, that is to say situated

14

within a story in the form of a plot and its peripities. Limiting ourselves to this perspective we can say, with Paul Veyne, that "to explain more requires telling it better." But what does it mean to explain more? It is here that the epistemological divide between scholarly history and the traditional story, which narrativist conceptions of historiography ignore, must be taken into account. With the introduction of "research-oriented history" (*histoire-recherche*), which François Furet contrasts with "narrative history" (*histoire-récit*), the explanatory form is made autonomous by becoming the stake of a game of authentification and justification; contributing to this process is, on the one hand, the enormous labor of conceptualization that is applied to the universals created by historical study (serfdom, the industrial revolution, etc.); on the other hand, there is the slicing up of a segment of the past into various levels (economic, social, political, intellectual, etc.) that must later be reconstituted within the limiting concept of total history; finally, there is the pluralization of historical time, of which Braudel's division into short-term, long-term, and quasi-immobile geographic time is one of the best illustrations. In all these activities a disparity is created between the level of naively narrative story-telling and the critical level of comprehensive explanation offered by professional historians. This is why I was able to assert that filiation on the basis of narrative understanding remained indirect.

In concluding this section it can be said that in spite of the manifold aspects of this epistemological separation, history continues to maintain a relationship of indirect filiation with the narrative form—this because even the least event-oriented historical discourse deals with temporal changes that affect human activity. By means of this indirect derivation narrative form gains explanatory value and takes its place within argumentative logic, which itself continues the *dispositio* of traditional rhetoric.

However, as mentioned above, the study of narrative form can not be limited to the epistemology of historical research; as a literary form it is already part of the writing of history. There is therefore a continuous back-and-forth between explanation and writing; or, to stay within the vocabulary of rhetorical categories, the narrative form is situated within the curve of *dispositio* and *elocutio*.

Paul Ricœur

The Writing of History and *elocutio*

It is indeed at this stage of rhetoric's intrusion into the field of historical theory that a host of new uncertainties and even grave theoretical difficulties arises. Exploiting them effectively and radically some contemporary authors have succeeded in turning the investigation of history as writing against the investigation of history as research; as a result the theory of history has broken loose from epistemology altogether to become part of the field of literary criticism.

An augur of this reversal was already visible in Mink's work: in his stress on the cognitive nature of narrative form (the title of Mink's last essay was "Narrative Form as a Cognitive Instrument") the distinction between history and fiction was blurred to the point of indistinguishability. History, it is said, strives to be a true story. But what are we to make of this claim if the narrative form of history is the only thing considered? What is in question here is the story's status as *representation* of the past. It is with this question that the problem of the writing of history really begins to be posed; and it is here that the conflict between *scientific* and *literary* criteria begins.

In this third stage of our study we are no longer dealing with rhetoric considered as a theory of argumentation: we are dealing with rhetoric as a theory of tropology. Earlier, in exploring this polarization of rhetoric, we found that the thread linking *inventio, dispositio,* and *elocutio* was broken. In large measure it was during the transition from the system of oral discourse to written discourse that *elocutio* was first freed from the broader rhetorical tradition, to be gradually narrowed until finally reduced to what Gérard Genette has called "limited rhetoric," (*rhétorique restreinte*), that is, limited to the pair metaphor-metonymy. But tropology itself had already established its own "limited rhetoric" within *elocutio*, in the same way that *elocutio* had given rise to an initial "limited rhetoric" in relation to a larger rhetorical system in which *inventio, dispositio,* and *elocutio* were part parts of a single discursive process.

Applied to the writing of history, the critique of rhetoric served as a weapon in the battle against what was deemed to be the naive representation of the past. This representation was considered a literary artifice whose hidden springs were to be revealed. What was absolutely new in all this was the polemical use to which rhetoric, now identified with ideological criticism, was subjected. In identifying rhetoric in this way it became a tool to be viewed with suspicion.

On the Anglo-Saxon side the decisive moment was the publication, in 1973, of Hayden White's book, *Metahistory, the Historical Imagination in XIXth Century Europe*, followed by *Tropics of Discourse* in 1978 and *The Content of the Form* in 1987. White calls this new approach metahistorical because it bears on interpretive strategies that govern the entire field of history, both the work of the philosophers of history (Hegel, Marx, Nietzsche, Croce) and its working historians (Michelet, Ranke, Tocqueville, Burckhardt). The point of departure for the investigation of this paradigm is fundamentally formalist; that is, the distinction between literary fiction and historiography is held to be of little importance; and the same holds for the distinction between historiography and the speculative philosophy of history. White begins by arranging, according to an ascending scale, the levels of conceptualization present in any work of history, under the assumption that beneath the first level lies nothing more than "the unprocessed historical record"; in other words data devoid of any order before history imprints its meaning on them—a meaning dependent on the paradigms detailed below. I will say nothing about the four paradigms that govern *emplotment*, nor about those regulating explanation by argument, nor those that guide explanation based on ideological implication. If we limited ourselves to these three levels *Metahistory* could still be harmonized with the narrativist approach in which story as such is treated as an explanatory mode. It is the last series of four paradigms that causes historical theory to tilt definitively in favor of literature over science. These paradigms, which no theorist before Hayden White took into consideration, derive directly from tropology: we are speaking of the four major tropes taken up by Ramus and Vico: metaphor, metonymy, synecdoche, and irony. For what reason does White grant such primacy to tropology? The answer to this question lies in a problematic element of narrativist theory that investigators like Mink brought to light without being about to solve it convincingly: that is, the ambition, which is the foundation of the distinction between history and fiction, to turn narrative structure into a model, an icon of the past, capable of *representing* it. How does tropology meet this challenge? The answer: "before a field can be interpreted it must first be constructed so that there is a ground inhabited by discernible figures." In order to present "what really happened" in the past, the historian must first *prefigure* the totality of events supplied by the documents. The function of this poetic activity is to trace, within "the historical field," all possible routes and thus give a preliminary profile to potential objects of knowledge. The design here is certainly directed toward retrieving what really happened in the past; the paradox is that this anterior state can not be identified without its being *prefigured*.

We can, in any case, question whether the reliance on tropology has not the inverse effect to the one sought; this being to explain the way in which history claims to represent the reality of the past. As a prefiguration of the historical field as such, the tropological approach denies any autonomous meaning to the idea of a real past invested with its own structure. Before the prefiguration there is no organized anything capable of being represented. The author is explicit: "It is by figuration that history forms a true subject of discourse." Here the idea of icon is sharply contrasted with that of model, in the sense that there is nothing originally given to which the model can be compared. To this idea another key concept is linked: "what gives a work of history its structure is not a careful reconstruction of the past but an act of poetic creativity." This last statement has far-ranging implications: in spite of White's insistence concerning the question of representation in history, it is not the faithfulness of that representation which interests him; it is the freedom of strategic choices that governs the organization of the field of history. For this reason the sub-title of *Metahistory* should not be forgotten: *the Historical Imagination in XIXth Century Europe* (Johns Hopkins University Press, 1973). In the final analysis the true glory of the imagination is its power of innovation. In this sense Hans Kellner, whose work will be discussed below, is correct in classing White in the great line of Renaissance humanists who, from Lorenzo Vala to Ramus and

18

then on to Vico, replaced logic with rhetoric. Now we can see why tropology wins out over explanation (even as a means of argument), why in tropology irony wins out over metaphor, and why *Metahistory* can be read entirely as an exercise in irony. However, one result of this transformation is that it becomes difficult to choose between two disparate readings of the system of paradigms governing the historical imagination; are we speaking here of a stable and closed system, as it is sometimes claimed, or rather being offered a manual to a game of unlimited combinations among the four tropes—a game leading to an endless process of deconstruction under the aegis of irony?

It is this second interpretation that dominates Hans Kellner's *Language and Historical Representation, Getting the Story Crooked* (University of Wisconsin Press, 1989). Rather than trying to solve the logical dilemma concerning the representation of the past, Kellner chooses to exacerbate it by further sharpening the rhetoric of suspicion that was used by Roland Barthes in his book "The Effect of Reality" (*L'effet du réel*).

The target of Kellner's attack is double: on the one hand is the belief "that there is a history out there that needs to be told"; on the other, the claim "that this history can be told straight by an honest and industrious historian using the correct method." Against the first presupposition the author has no difficulty in restating the oft-repeated assertion that history does not exist until it is constructed and written. He shows more originality in asserting that language and its *rhetoric* constitute another source—along with archival and computer-generated materials—and that this other source brings something different than order to historical invention. With this assertion one of the basic axioms of the narrativist school of history is challenged head-on: the setting in motion of the plot is not equivalent to the establishment of order. Rather, the ideas of complete form, of coherence and closure, are themselves suspect claims whose only real defense is the anxiety generated by the idea of disorder. There is, as Foucault asserted as well, something willed and ultimately regressive in the imposition of order. The argument in favor of discontinuity begins at the initial stage, with the consideration of the document, which the archive had endowed with a halo of authority. It is not only that the debris of the past is scattered; so is the testimony to that past. Moreover, the field of documentation itself adds its own effects of "selective destruction" to the other ways by which supposed historical "evidence" is distorted through the loss of information. Rhetoric is therefore not something added to the documentation: it is part of it from the start. Here one might hope that the narrative form itself could provide an antidote to the anguish provoked by the lacunas in the documentary evidence. However, for its part the story form gives rise to new anxieties tied to other discontinuities. It is here that White's approach to tropology enters the picture. The tropological reading, it is said, is only "bothersome"—and therefore a source of new anxiety—if a new system, based on White's four tetrads, fails to be constructed over it. The so-called "bedrock of order" must itself be understood as an allegorical game in which irony is acknowledged as the master trope inside the system as well as the overall point of view of the system. Ultimately all tropology is ironic, pledged to the thousand "turns" that allow linguistic structures to create meaning. White can therefore be suspected of having retreated, with a mixture of sympathy and ... anxiety, in the face of what he calls, at the end of *Tropics of Discourse*, "the absurdist moment." This systematic application of tropology is equivalent to a synechdochic treatment (whole/part) of irony itself, which must remain the all-purpose trope. While rhetoric was supposed to destabilize logic, the final result is "a volontarist rhetoric that restrains a deconstructive antilogic." But if this deconstructive antilogic is given into, the destructive progression of tropological inflation appears to become limitless. And once the figures of discourse themselves become figures of thought, tropology itself becomes virtually irrelevant. Moreover, there seems to be little left for historians to learn from a critical enterprise that seeks not to uncover dissimulated chaos disguised as order, but rather one in which the historian's craft, as an institutionalized discipline as such, is treated as a willful and organized resistance to the very enterprise of "getting the story crooked". Paradoxically, the defender of rhetoric here finds him or herself in a situation comparable to that of the defender of the *covering law model*; while the latter tried to tell the historian how to write history, the former now tells the defender of rhetoric how history itself can no longer be written. If the philosophy of history has turned away from the workplace in which the contemporary historian labors, is it not because rhetoric, occupying the entire field, has claimed for itself the phases of both documentary research and explanation? When everything is rhetoric the question of truth evaporates, and with it historical reality. This is done by assigning to the defenders of historical reality the simplistic thesis that the past, in order to be real, must have the form of a story waiting to be told. At the end of this article I will try to outline a concept for the reality of the past in which what has really happened does not require a pre-existent narrative form in order to be known.

For the time being I will rely on the spontaneous realism of the historian, the kind implicit in what can be called the intentionality of historical consciousness. The strategy of suspicion, which is employed by both the proponents of the "effect of reality" and by those authors desirous of "getting the story crooked," is equivalent to treating the historian as such as an illusion-maker, at times even an explorer seized with panic at the idea of venturing onto shaky ground. I will oppose to this perverted understanding of rhetoric those aspects of the intentionality of historical consciousness that tend to justify the historian's inclination to take his constructions for reconstructions of something that once was and no longer is.

To start, however, I must take exception to the kind of definition of historical realism to which the opponents of historical realism try to limit its defenders. Either, they say, the past is an *untold story*, or it is a formless chaos until the story itself exists. This presumed—and extremely crude—definition of realism depends on the predication of a direct correspondence between the past and its representation; in the worst case this correspondence is assumed to be one of image to copy, in the best case a projection similar to a cartographer's, obeying rules of transposition that are in fact undiscoverable. The real challenge, in my view, is to reformulate in more subtle terms the historian's spontaneous realism, while keeping in mind the perfectly justified rejection of the truth-as-correspondence thesis as applied to the representation of the past. There exists, beyond the pair *untold story* / formlessness, a third solution, one that seems to be spontaneously presumed by historical intentionality itself, without however being consciously adopted by it. I am referring to the presupposition that history has for its subject people like you and me, who act and suffer within circumstances that they themselves did not create, and with results both desired and undesired. This presupposition links historical theory to a theory of action. Inverting the same presupposition, we can say that human action requires, in order to be understood, a story that will uncover its fundamental connections. We can thus agree with Hannah Arendt in saying that it is the *story's* duty to express the "who" of action; or, more broadly, with Paul Veyne, to say that history articulates the plot of action by coordinating intentions, causes and accidents. The path linking history to action can thus be traveled in either direction: from story to action, to the extent that story—according to Aristotle's formulation—is *mimesis praxeôs*; or from action to story, to the extent that action is, in one way or another, a demand for story.

This first response to the antirealist attack—an attack based on treating rhetoric as a weapon to be viewed with suspicion—still leaves unresolved the enigma associated with the what-was-and-no-longer-is, which is the literal mystery of the past. At the very least it can be asserted that the terms "past" applies to an event of acting-suffering that transcends the alternative *untold story* / the indeterminate. What is past is a particular field of praxis, invested with structures dependent on a theory of action. What remains to be specified is the nature of the relationship between historians writing about the past and the past quality of the acting-suffering of human beings who have acted and suffered as we do.

A second answer can now be given, although it will remain merely formal at this stage of the discussion. The historian, it can be said, exists in the same spatio-temporal framework as does the object of his study. History, it has not often enough been pointed out, is one of the rare modes of knowledge in which the subject and object belong not only to the same practical field but to the same temporal one as well. Although we are here only referring to the chronological aspect of historiography, it remains true that in order for an event to be considered historic it must be dateable. Whatever the character—constructed or reconstructed—of the sequence of events of a particular period, the very same system is used to date the three temporal events that constitute the period under consideration; that is, the beginning of the period under consideration, its end or conclusion, and the present of the historian (more precisely, of the historical enunciation). Thanks to this single system of dating, which includes the historical object and the historian subject, both the events whose trail (*trace*) is found in the documents, and the event that consists in recounting these tracks or traces, are assumed to take place in the same universe as the occurrences studied by the natural sciences. This implicit conviction is an important component of the historian's realism.

A third step in the direction of what might be called a critical realism of historical knowledge can be taken by observing that historiography is itself a praxis. Thus Michel de Certeau speaks of "historical activity" in order to designate the operation that consists of "making history." However, this present activity has a complex relationship to the activity of the people of the past who themselves "made history." Along with formal adherence to a single spatio-temporal framework linking the historian's activity to the same system of dating as the events being described, we can also speak of material adherence to a single field of praxis, evidenced by the historian's dependence on the "making" of real historical actors for his own history "making." Before presenting themselves as master craftsmen of stories made out of the past, historians must first stand as heirs to the past. This idea of inheritance presupposes that the past in some sense lives in the present and therefore affects it. It is this passive dimension of historical inheritance that is best expressed by the idea of historical *debt*. Before even forming the idea of re-presenting the past, we are in debt to the men and women of the past who contributed to making us what we are. Before we can represent the past we must live as beings affected by the past.

This notion of debt allows us to revive the notion of track or trail (*trace*), whose implications for history Marc Bloch implicitly acknowledged when he defined history as "knowledge by tracks." The relationship between a track and the thing of which it is a trace is not that of copy or cartographic projection: rather it is the vicarious function of standing-in-place-of (*lieu-tenance*), which the German language skillfully expresses by distinguishing between *Vertretung* (representation, substitution) and *Vorstellung* (presentation, idea). *Vorstellung* is the mental image that the subject creates of an absent thing. *Vertretung* is the relationship by means of which a representative takes the place of the thing represented in its absence. Such is the case with a trace. The indirectness of the referent inherent in the relationship of history to the past is characteristic of this vicarious function.

* * *

This defense of the referential function of history leads me to express the relationship between history and rhetoric in the following terms. It was a by a kind of perversion that tropology was made to serve an ideological critique that interpreted the desire to please as a desire to seduce and deceive. This inflation of tropology was a result of the uprising of tropology against argumentation; yet argumentation should have remained the center of gravity of the epistemology of history. Finally, the preeminent role of argumentation can only be restored if explanation itself is not separated from the search for documentary evidence. Thus we find ourselves bound to retrace in reverse order the sequence of the great rhetorical tradition: from *elocutio* to *inventio* by way of *dispositio*. Only by so doing can rhetoric remain, as Aristotle wanted it, the "antistrophe" of dialectic in the sense of a logic of the probable.

Translated by Thomas Epstein

Notes

1. Kristofz Pomian. *L'Ordre du Temps* (Paris, 1984) 33.
2. Paul Veyne. *Comment on écrit l'histoire* (Paris, 1979).

Scholarship and the Responsibility of the Historian

Christian Meier

We can hardly know for certain how strongly a scholarly discipline like history is able to affect politics and society, popular views and morals. Whatever its impact, it's influence also varies from epoch to epoch. During a few decades of the nineteenth century, historians were overwhelmed by so many questions and by such high expectations that there existed a large public space for them that they merely had to occupy. At other times, they have had to conquer this space first if they wanted to gain continued attention.

To be sure, a differentiation has to be introduced: any society has particular interests, e.g., in parts of its more recent past or in events that society sees as having something like a "mythical quality" about then, events that represent a major divide, that are deeply imprinted on that society's memory, that have attained a special role through tradition. There is, of course, always a space commanding wider public attention for these aspects. However, they are no more than small specks on the large canvas of history.

Still, however receptive the public may be to the historian's work, it is safe to assume that historical scholarship *can* have influence. Ideas, views, and opinions are being formed-among politicians, journalists, and entire societies-on the basis of instruction in school, of the reading of history books and other traces left by historical scholarship. The self-images of entire societies, the claims of nations, the perception of other nations, but also the conviction that a particular order is the right one or that societal conditions are problematical as well as a myriad of other factors, are derived, inter alia, from history, from a history that is rather more accurately interpreted at certain times and misinterpreted at others.

Christian Meier

Historical scholarship can play an enhancing or an inhibiting role in this process; it can be useful or can cause damage, and will do so intentionally or inadvertently. Historical scholarship can offer too much or too little, it can be either too verbose or too taciturn with regard to questions that happen to be topical; naturally, it can also be too accommodating or too reserved toward certain contemporary trends. Historical scholarship can miss out on fighting myths, misunderstandings, and errors, and can fail to counter falsifications. But it can also direct the public's attention to what has been forgotten or repressed. Historical scholarship can thus be the source of many influences remain mute.

During the 1960s a violent debate raged in the Federal Republic of Germany on whether the German Empire's share of responsibility in the outbreak of World War I was very much higher than had been assumed. In this case the results of historical research have badly shaken the image of a "good" and "decent" pre-1933 Germany to which the Germans so much liked to cling after the horrendous crimes of the Nazi period. And the opposition was accordingly vigorous. The public became strongly involved. The doubts about Bismarck's work had by then become so powerful that the one hundredth anniversary of the founding of the German Empire could not be celebrated in 1971. Later, a peculiar connection sprang up between new interpretations of the Bismarckian empire on the one hand, and the change of parliamentary power in Bonn on the other. Yet another turn in events occurred in 1989. The debate on the extermination of the European Jews and other groups was particularly heated in the wake of the film "Holocaust" in 1979; but the debate was also conducted in the general public independently of this film and with varying intensity throughout the postwar period, with historians playing a prominent part in it. It was an involvement that had manifold consequences-extending as far as the *Historikerstreit* of 1986/88 which was extraordinarily passionate and whose repercussions can be felt to this day. Other examples could be cited from other countries.

Historiography, moreover, has access to a myriad of human experiences, of varieties of political and social life, action, suffering, conservation, and transformation. It can use them to "test" the most diverse sets of questions; it can conduct a kind of retro-

26

spective experiment and draw from this an array of conclusions that may have far-reaching consequences.

All this supports the notion that the historian must give an account of the possible effects (or non-effects) of his work; that he must ask himself above all, what kinds of obligations toward his time grow from his knowledge and his opportunities, or to put it differently, from his vocation.

This question becomes all the more urgent owing to circumstance that some people like to advance against the actuality of historical scholarship, i.e., that the age in which we live has become far removed from all history and that this distance is growing all the time because of ever more rapid change. This is frequently illustrated by reference to the fact that the number of the living is larger today than that of all who have ever died. But it is precisely the relative distance of the present from (nearly) all things past that is responsible for the extraordinary degree of our lack of orientation. This carries with it great risks at the same time, as everything is in a state of flux. If there is no intervention things will not stay as they are, but they will change without there being any possibility of control. On the one hand, a huge number of things-even genes-appear to becoming under human control; on the other hand, the effects and side-effects of these actions turn into processes which are not easy to completely master; and the changes that result from this are meanwhile capable of calling into question essential preconditions of human life on earth for some time to come.

All kinds of different rules and axioms fail. For many things that require urgent attention there exist as yet no rules and axioms.

If this is so, then the historians, like other scholars, must ask themselves whether they have a contribution to make toward providing an orientation in the present, in particular, and overall. The conclusions that the various participants in the present age draw from this are in the end, of course, of a political nature, not a scholarly one. But much has already been gained if the problems we face are at least better known and if material is made available that helps to make it easier to come to a judgment.

What was implied by the old maxim—*historia magistra vitae*—was that politicians could learn from history and apply this to their policies in a world scarcely confronted with structural problems. A second motif of ancient historiography was to make it easier for readers to bear fateful setbacks; to bear up under history. As indicated above, the contribution of historical writing seems to lie today in providing orientation within a large variety of problems and connections. Historians are by no means the only ones charged with this task; but they can presumably make a contribution that no other person can so readily provide.

In short, the historian does have a responsibility; it is a responsibility toward his contemporaries and future generations, to whom this world will one day be given over. It is, by the way, also a responsibility toward the dead, but this is a problem that will be put aside here.

This responsibility may be defined—as always in such cases in terms of an "as-if"—as if much depended on the individual in his field and indeed in fields considerably removed. Without overestimating ourselves, we must nevertheless act as if our own actions do make a difference.

The next question to ask is what are the consequences if this responsibility is taken seriously. In this context we shall have to ignore what the individual may deem necessary on the basis of his historical work, though not without its framework, for example in politics, in partisan organizations, in the shape of a large variety of recommendations and statements. Such activities are a personal matter; they transcend scholarship. To be sure, in individual cases they may be difficult to separate from a person's scholarship, and it works in both directions: practice is of course also reflected in scholarship, just as scholarship in some way tends to influence practice. However, our task here is merely to define what basic rules might be established for history as a scholarly discipline. I would differentiate here between three aspects:

1) The scholarly work of the individual in teaching and research;

2) The general orientation of teaching and research in history as a discipline;

3) The ways in which one turns toward the more general public.

The Individual's Scholarship in Teaching and Research

Leopold von Ranke once took the view that scholarship must intervene in life. This he thought to be unquestionably true. However, in order to have an effect, historiography above all had to be a science. "We can," he wrote, "have a true impact on the present only if we disregard the latter for the moment and elevate ourselves to free, objective science." I would consider this to be fundamentally correct, even if we may have doubts about the extent of objectivity that we can achieve.

"Disregarding the present" may merely mean, however, that the practical interests the historian pursues in the present should not influence his work. His theoretical, observing interests, on the other hand, may certainly be geared toward the present, because he learns from his age which makes certain questions, for example, more accessible to him; and it is these that in turn enable him to decipher the period that he looks at, not least some of its peculiarities.

All historical work draws on the present at least for its language; moreover, current language is being used to distinguish between what is and is not self-evident, which in turn determines the discourse in different ways. Finally, there are questions, views, examples and other things. Ideally and over time the experience of very diverse epochs-whether martial or peaceful, stagnant or dynamic, stable or revolutionary, etc.-should accumulate. What is more likely to happen, however, is that each generation makes a fresh start.

In any case, historians tend to be closer to certain historical epochs, and more remote from others, on account of the quality of their own epoch. This becomes particularly clear *ex post facto* and with the benefit of hindsight. Much of what is conditioned by the present in historical research appears to be unconscious, and there is hence always the danger of falling victim to certain contemporary trends.

I would like to assert that the responsibility of the historian demands that he observe his own epoch *very consciously*. This enables him, on the one hand, to approach with more distance and hence more critically the insinuations that offer themselves through the experiences of his age; on the other hand, conscious observation multiplies the cognitive gains that can be made. Finally, it enables him to test, in reference to historical topics, questions that emerge from the present and thus to explicate them more clearly, in the hope of perhaps also making a contribution to an understanding of the present.

Thus the interest in micro-history that has emerged from certain very specific contemporary experiences in our time and its needs can also open up many topics from more distant periods. The temptation in this case is that we elaborate on differences between the present and the recent past not just in the individual case, but also with regard to the whole. In this way the problem gets caught up in broader contexts. If we take this approach, it is likely to happen that we encounter the question of the relationship between micro- and macro-history, and this may be very different from one society to another, simultaneously posing the challenge to look at the peculiarity of the modern situation with fresh eyes.

To give a second example: the modern question of what constitutes the collective identity of societies, e.g., of nations, opens up the peculiarities of the "identity of the citizen" if applied to ancient Athens. If we then compare the two concepts, we can make observations that may be the starting-point for further reflections in matters of "identity" and its modern problematic. Citizens' identity was rather a closed idea, that assumed a far-reaching homogeneity among the citizenry, while at the same time promoting this sameness. National identity is determined by the fact (and also occasionally very susceptible to the fact) that it tries to bridge many profound differences and antagonisms in a society that as a whole is also very much larger than its Athenian counterpart. It was part of the citizens' identity to be largely focused on the present. National identity, by contrast, is often linked to expectations for the future and, indeed, of progress, and it is perhaps also for this reason that it is more and more firmly grounded in some more distant past. At the very least national identity has a lot to with history and with the formation of historical myths. It would be intriguing-and topical-to ask to what extent the value of work that is often very differently assessed has a place in this view of identity that is also partly its own justification.

To cite a third example: this is the observation that different parts of the world, but increasingly Europe as well, are experiencing a weakening of the power with which state authority penetrates societies; Mafia organizations proliferate as partial structures of domination. These developments are not only reviving an interest in many characteristics of the early modern period, of the middle ages, and of antiquity, but may also provide an incentive to think more deeply and-by reference of historical analysis-about the preconditions of state authority as well its functional equivalents during other ages. How can a functioning political unity be generated? How can it secure, beyond and above particularist interests, the unity of the formation of the political will; and how can it assert this will? How can this be done if, on top of it all, we have the granting of manifold liberties, possibly even within a democratic framework?

If I may mention two details from my own work, such questions can even throw new light on Greek and Roman history. My starting point is a rough differentiation between two kinds of "solidarity"-one horizontal and the other vertical. "Vertical solidarity" refers to relationships between those "upstairs" (usually politicians) and those "downstairs." The latter support the former in order secure the formers' power. In return those "upstairs" grant personal advantages to those "downstairs." This is a relationship in which particularist interests are being served above all. Looking at the whole of world history, this appears to be an almost natural situation. If you scratch my back, I'll scratch yours. Everyone gains something. The question is how common interest may be defended in these circumstances.

The Roman Republic was permeated in thousands of ways by "vertical solidarities"; or to be precise, by clientelism. These solidarities were complemented by friendships among more or less equals. The practice of noble rule was the essential element. However, within the nobility (within the Senate, to be exact) we can observe strong elements of a "horizontal solidarity" that to some extent took the vertical solidarities into their service, and in any case restricted their impact. There existed in this respect a certain discipline, a strong capacity to reach a consensus, that was buttressed institutionally. Attican democracy, on the other hand, succeeded in virtually excluding vertical solidarities. Horizontal solidarity was so powerful here that the unity of the polis was in fact based on the solidarity of its broad strata of citizens. There was a mutual agreement to defend and preserve certain common interests.

If we turn this question around and apply it to our age, it becomes very clear that modern democracies (and societies) cannot function, inside and outside the parties, without manifold vertical solidarities. Certain elements of modern statehood-the legacy of the absolutist monarchies-may still act as a counterweight up to a point. But the more these elements are removed, the more we face the question of how far they can be countered by horizontal solidarities, how far as a consequence of this our democracies will be pressed to provide even greater supports.

There is no space here to go into this. Nor is it impossible that such observations might be reached on quite different paths. But in my judgment there is much to be said for the assumption that the means of human cognition are limited, and that we must hence exploit every opportunity to augment them. To reiterate, what applies here is the "as-if."

These and many other questions can influence and enrich historical work in many different ways. For instance, to stay with my example, when applied in connection with the political order of Rome or Athens or certain phases of their histories. But they can also be the stimulus for larger projects, for entire books.

Thus one of the fundamental treatments of "Greeks and Barbarians," the subject of Julius Jüttner's 1923 study, represents, as the author remarks in his preface, a response to the experience of World War I, to the "shameful fact ... that the outbreak of hostilities among the nations killed at a stroke all sense of human solidarity and generated a flaming hatred among some that could not do enough to denigrate the enemy."

It is conceivable that today the problem of the great migrations (the emergence and growth of minorities that cannot be assimilated or are unwilling to assimilate) may stimulate fresh research. Here, too, questions that have been opened up by the present lead to observations relating to Greek democracy. In general terms it may be said that the more democratically a city was organized, the more carefully it watched over keeping the circle of citizens small and sealed from the outside world. How far is democracy therefore dependent on "homogeneity?" I shall leave aside the questions that follow from this question. Nor is it possible to answer modern questions by using antiquity as one's starting point. And yet it seems plausible that we may be able to throw additional light on these questions if we approach them from the perspective of ancient history; that by studying them it becomes possible to formulate them more sharply. Once again the difference between polis and nation would have to be considered, in addition to the difference between old and new nations in the modern period and perhaps also in addition to the problem of a Europe that is growing together. I do not wish to maintain that by doing this even late antiquity may turn out to be a topical subject; however, it is not completely without interest in the broader (!) context of these questions.

And finally, the theme of "violence," of its genesis and of the preconditions of fighting it, may assume a completely new aspect from the perspective of our time. Detached historical contemplations could, in turn, facilitate observations that may be capable of contributing to our current understanding of violence, and the problem of "horizontal solidarity" would have to be given prominent consideration in the process. It is an odd experience that nevertheless forces itself upon you with regard both to the history of science and to the present state of science: if there is a strong cognitive interest that is guided by the present, the questions with which one approaches history are also different.

No doubt this gives rise to the danger that a subject is wrongly turned into something topical. But this danger will be lessened the more we are conscious of these questions and of our own present. There is also the danger that interested laymen in politics and the media will try to use historical insights for their purposes. The more topical these insights are, the more tempting this will be. This will be inevitable. But in this respect, too, I would like to assert that reflecting upon the historian's responsibility offers the best antidote. The more a discipline insists on this responsibility, the more difficult it will be to pursue political tendencies within the context of science. The yardsticks must be clear. And the international scientific community will see to it that these yardsticks will be adhered to.

The General Orientation of Research and the Discipline of History

Second, responsibility toward the present seems to make it imperative that the scholarly discourse among historians must undergo change, or to be more precise: the ways we give attention to divergent potential topics and the ways in which access to the subject is regulated for college and high school students.

I am afraid that we will not be able to organize our living together into a more forcefully united Europe and on a planet that has become very small if we, i.e., the members of the different nations, do not know more about each other. To begin with, the task is to create in historiography above all, but not only in this field, preconditions for the development of an "intercultural competence." We must clarify our thoughts to a much larger degree than we have done so far about the images that we have about each other; and this invariably involves referring to history. But we must also try, again via history, to gain better access to each other. This is presumably difficult enough in western and central Europe, not to mention the Balkans and the countries of the former Soviet Union.

I also think that in the future historiography must in some way turn its attention more seriously to the histories of the Arab and Indian, Chinese, Japanese-and perhaps also the Korean- worlds as well as those of different parts of Africa. It may be no more than a minor blemish that a discipline that calls itself "History" ordinarily only deals with the development of Europe and North America and that the rest of the world appears only in so far as it was somehow affected by Europe. True, we have a number of specialists to cover the histories of the Asian and African peoples, and in some countries, like France, for example, there are more of them, while their number in others, like Germany, is smaller. But even in Germany that figure is slowly increasing. Yet must historical research into classical Occidental antiquity not also take account African and Asian history? Can we afford a situation in which historians at best have a coincidental knowledge of those fields? Most importantly, is it still tolerable today that we see our own history essentially from the inside and without fully realizing how strange it must appear to the members of other non-European societies? And without appreciating the full extent to which it is peculiar?

The peculiarities of societies (and in particular of certain epochs in the history of these societies) have increasingly become a topic of historiography. All inquiries into historical subjects, consciously or unconsciously, delineate these themes from others. All important historical analyses are marked by certain underlying assumptions about the spectrum of anthropological possibilities of which one happens to be realized in a particular case in point. This means that we must also include to a far larger extent those possibilities that we encounter in Asia and Africa.

How this might be achieved is a difficult question. Jacob Burckhardt has remarked:

> In the sciences ... we can only claim to master one limited branch, i.e., as a specialist, and somehow this is what one *should* be. However, if we do not want to lose the capacity to possess a general overview, we should also be dilettantes with respect to as many other fields as possible, at least on our own account in order to increase our knowledge and to enrich ourselves in our perspectives; otherwise we remain, with regard to everything that lies beyond our specialism, an ignoramus and possible even a very uncouth fellow.

At any rate, it is not sufficient that many historians know a lot about limited aspects of history; all historians should be knowledgeable about more than their specialized fields, or to be more precise: they should know something about divergent histories, including those outside their specialisms and more particularly about histories outside their own culture.

Next to ever more far-reaching specialization and, indeed, in opposition to it we should create and reinforce a trend toward "Generalization." It may sound sacrilegious, but the question must be allowed as to whether it is really appropriate that we historians usually devote ourselves to such an extent to specialized and even ever more specialized research. Much of this is no doubt very important and fruitful; the last decades have shown, not least in France, what significant new insights can be gained even in our age; no one would wish to miss these insights; there is no indication that this kind of work is going to disappear, and specialization clearly will have to remain.

However, next to it there is room for a more generalizing approach, for example à la Max Weber; it makes sense and may even be necessary, even if it may impose, in a few cases, certain restrictions on more specialized activities.

Thus there is the question as to whether the histories of Africa and Asia should be given more space and above all a place of their own in the school curricula so that they are no longer merely seen as a function in the context of European history. Would it not be possible to have a requirement for students of history to enroll at least in one more detailed course introducing them to the histories of Africa and Asia? Should we not try to integrate historians of other civilizations more into the general teaching and research of history, for instance, through seminars with a comparative angle that deal with individual problems of politics, economics, religion, mentality and so on within divergent societies and epochs? On the one hand, this would open up many fresh perspectives for all parts of historiography; on the other, it would promote historical "expertise," i.e., an understanding of different shapes that political organizations, parties, labor relations or dependencies and even gender relations may assume in different societies. We encounter but few of these formations in our own work and are therefore easily inclined to see them as absolute. What this really means is that we do not know enough about them; that we must learn more about them.

There is no question that reforms of this kind would not only benefit historical scholarship, even down to the detail, but would also be important both for our treatment of foreign nations and for an understanding of what is happening among us Europeans today. There is no need to elaborate on this.

An expansion of historical study that is gained in this way would require manifold contacts and cooperations with other disciplines, e.g, political science, economics, law, sociology, anthropology, and religious studies. Nevertheless, a clear demarcation line would remain between them and historiography. The historian would continue to do what he is ideally most capable of, i.e., through the study of sources, through analysis, but also in the way he provides syntheses for different epochs, synchronically as well as diachronically. It will also remain indispensable that each historian has his own special fields, has gained his qualifications in them and is at home in them-if only in order to test in his own field all those questions that emerge from the discussions in different sub-disciplines and from those with other subjects; enabling him to make his contribution to the general discourse in an "expert" manner.

As a rule, what the other disciplines need from historiography can, as a rule, not be drawn from older, long published textbooks (although this happens quite frequently and with questionable results); rather it must time and again be created anew and on the basis of questions that are currently being posed. Often this may also then lead to the discovery of fresh sources. This generally results in gains for those who ask these questions as well as those (the historians in this case) who answer them, making modifications in the process-for all disciplines and perhaps even beyond.

Modes of Transmission to the General Public

Finally, there is the third aspect—the face presented the outside world, the desire to inform wider circles about history, and non-historians in particular. Much is usually happening in this field, in essays and monographs or in grand surveys of entire epochs or histories.

A few matters deserve mention in this context. To begin with, there is the problem of consciously trying to put across an idea of the different parts of human existence that are being covered. We live fairly abstract lives today; compared to earlier generations our experiences are much less direct. Often we are also isolated. The prosperity that we have been able to enjoy during the period of our history that is just behind us has also caused us not to miss such experiences too much. Developments that have moved the history of mankind for thousands of years and that remained on the agenda outside the western and northern half of the globe, were deemed by us to be hardly conceivable anymore.

Karl Kraus remarked as early as 1914 that the unimaginable was occurring all the time; and that it would not happen if it were imaginable. Hannah Arendt wrote in 1960 that Eichmann was incapable of *imagining* what he had *done* ("Eichmann habe sich nicht *vorstellen* können, was er *anstellte*"). Historical writing is well-suited to redressing our lack of imagination. At the same time there is the question of how far this capacity can reach, if the present provides but few bridges. Still, the attempt must in my view be made.

It also seems to me that the responsibility of the historian requires deeper reflection on what is required with respect to historical synthesis. The old problem of partiality presents itself in a new guise-and not just regarding the historian's relationship with individual leaders, nations, religions, with those "upstairs" and those "downstairs," with bourgeoisie and proletariat, for example. We can also take sides between men and women, perhaps even without realizing it, and between the majority and various minorities. Earlier on there was merely the danger that one sided with the winners or the losers; the question now is as to whether we have adequately taken into account the soldiers next to their commander or the victims next to the survivors. Whereas the glories and achievements of an epoch once attracted a lot of attention, we now ask at the same time whether sufficient thought has been given to the costs, the use of resources; and this use does not merely concern the air we breathe, the climate, trees, flora and fauna; it also involves the entire and complex field of what, in short, might be called mentality.

However, as we know today, it may also be a consequence of certain perhaps even unconscious decisions that the historian has made, if he highlights or de-emphasizes the role of personalities, or events, or structures and more or less autonomous processes. In this respect, too, there arises a need to reflect and to take stock; for it is not important what kind of picture is being transmitted of human potentialities and limitations.

The task is, especially in writings on the more recent past, to consider divergent possibilities of identification that demand their place in historical analysis. To refer to just the most extreme example: the history of the extermination of the European Jews must deal not only with the actual perpetrators and victims, but also with other participants of various kinds with varying degrees of involvement. We must deal with the victims as well as the survivors; with those who complied and those who resisted. History must try to describe from a distant as well as a close-up perspective-and there are also parts about which it must remain silent.

The gist of my deliberations might be summarized as follows: historians, like everyone else, clearly have in their own way a responsibility toward their own age and its future. They should be conscious of this. They should mutually promote and reinforce this responsibility. The responsibility can pertain only to the performance of their scholarship, thereby reinforcing not only its significance, but also its fruitfulness. Above all, it is urgent that this responsibility be assumed for it is no longer possible to go on as before.

The Social Function of History

Enrique Florescano

"There is not, then, more than one science of man in time (history), and that science has the task of uniting the study of the dead with the study of the living."

— Marc Bloch[1]

Unlike the scientist, who in the nineteenth century was anointed with the aura of the solitary genius, the historian has, since ancient times, been thought of as a creator conditioned by his social group. The historian knows his profession thanks to routine apprenticeship under his professors. He trains in the discipline by reading the models inherited from his predecessors. He discovers the secrets of the art by analyzing the work of his colleagues. His richest sources of inspiration are the masterpieces of all times from the most diverse cultures.

The challenges imposed on him by his professional colleagues, as well as the current inescapable competition under which he suffers, are the incentives that induce him to improve himself. That is to say, from the time he chooses his vocation until he learns to carry it out, he is surrounded by inescapable social conditioning. On the one hand, he is a social product, the result of diverse collective actions; on the other hand, he is an individual driven by the desire to overcome the legacy of the past and to transform his profession by responding to the challenges of the present.

If we could transport ourselves into the different ages of the past, and draw from this images showing the functions that our ancestors assigned to rescuing the past, we would see that the tasks of history have varied. One could also notice that those tasks have been concentrated around the purpose of endowing groups of human beings with identity, cohesion, and collective consciousness.

Since ancient times the peoples that inhabited the land we now call Mexico resorted to recollections of the past to combat the

destructive influence of time upon human foundations; to knit solidarities based on common origins; to legitimate the possession of
territory; to affirm identities rooted in remote traditions; to sanc-
tion established power; to validate with the prestige of the past
the vindications of the present; to base in a shared past the aspira-
tion of constructing a nation; or to give support to projects directed
at the uncertainty of the future.[2]

In all these cases, the function of the historical record is to
endow the diverse human beings that formed the tribe, the people, the fatherland, or the nation with an identity. The recovery of
the past had as its ends the creation of shared social values, instill-
ing the idea that the group or the nation had a common origin, as
well as the inculcation of the conviction that the similarity of origins lent cohesion to the diverse members of the social group—a
cohesion that enabled these people to face the difficulties of the
present and take on the challenges of the future with confidence.

To endow a people or a nation with a common past, and to
forge in this remote origin a collective identity, is perhaps the most
ancient and most constant of history's social functions. It was
invented long ago and remains active today. As John Updike, who
remains the tribal specialist with the task of telling others what
each group needs to know, says: "Who are we? What were our origins? Who were our ancestors? How did we arrive at this point or
this crossroads in history?"[3]

This primordial function explains the great attraction that the
historical account has, as well as its vast, diverse, and continually
redoubled audience. It attracts most people's curiosity because
historical accounts transport the reader to the mysterious place of
origins and has about it the seductiveness of travel to remote
places. Another attraction of historical narratives is its suggestion
of offering a clarification of the beginnings of the group and thus
drawing us closer to our ancestors. By building a bridge between
the remote past and the uncertain present, the historical account
performs the function of creating a relationship of kinship with
ancestors near and distant, a feeling of continuity within the
group, people, or nation.

But if on the one hand history makes us enter into the identities
of the group and the search for what is our own, on the other it

forces us to recognize the diversity of human experience by opening up in us a recognition of the other; in this manner history makes us participants in experiences not lived, but with which we identify and form our sense of the plurality of human adventure.

For the student of history, immersion in the past is a constantly astonishing encounter with different ways of life influenced by different environments and cultures. Because of these special brush strokes of historical knowledge, history could be called the profession of understanding. It requires that we understand the actions and motivations of people different from ourselves. And as this task is accomplished with groups and people who are no longer present, it is also an exercise in understanding the exotic.

We can thus say that studying the past presupposes an openness to other human beings. It requires us to transport ourselves to other times, to know places never before seen, to familiarize ourselves with living conditions different from our own. In other words, the job of the historian demands a curiosity toward knowledge of the other, an inclination toward wonderment, an openness to the different, and the practice of tolerance.

It is true that not all historians display a sympathy and inclination for the unusual. But the bulk of participants in the profession, and some of its most distinguished masters, reveal that the practice of the historian, when carried out with probity, is an openness to understanding and an inclination for the remote and exotic.

At the same time as the historical imagination strives to revive what has disappeared or give permanence to what is little by little disappearing, on the other hand it is also inquiring into the inescapable transformation of the lives of individuals, groups, societies and states. It has been said that history is the study of individual and social change over time.

A good number of the tools historians have developed to understand the past detect change and transformation. We study the momentary and almost imperceptible change that the passing of the time provokes in our lives. We analyze the formidable impact of conquests, revolutions and the political and social explosions that dislocate ethnicities, classes, peoples, and nations. And in the same vein we have created refined methods to study slow changes that over the course of hundreds and thousands of years transform geography, economic structures, mentalities, or institutions. Thanks to the analysis of these diverse moments in time, the study of history has imposed the task of living while being conscious of the brevity of individual existence, of the awareness that our actions today rest on past experience and will extend into the future, of the conviction that we are part of the great stream of history, of a greater current along which flow nations, civilizations, and the components of the human race. By reconstructing the memory of past deeds, history fulfills a fundamental human need: it integrates the lives of individuals into the collective current of life.

On the other hand, when historical investigation analyzes the diverse events of the past, it is obligated to consider each one of them on its own terms, which are specifically the values of the time and place where it occurred. By proceeding with this criterion of authenticity, the historian grants these experiences their own significance and lasting value. In this manner, history becomes the instrument by which past actions acquire a unique meaning in general human development. In this way, individual experiences and acts born of the most withdrawn intimacy become undying testimony, human footprints that do not age or devalue in the passing of time.

Centuries ago, on observing this characteristic of historical recovery, the humanist Marsilio Ficino wrote: "History is necessary not only to make life pleasant, but also to confer upon it a moral sense. What is, in itself, mortal, gains immortality in history; what is found absent becomes present; the old is rejuvenated."[4]

On the other hand, the incessant revision that history performs upon the issues that most obsess human beings makes them relative, stripping them of the absolute value that at one time it had attempted to endow them with. Against the absolutist pretensions of those who advocate a single church, state, or social order for all humanity, history shows, with the force of human experience over the centuries, that nothing that has existed in the course of social development is definitive or eternal. Hornung warns that history: "inexorably destroys all the 'eternal' and 'absolute' values and shows the relativity of the absolute references that we struggle to establish."[5] On contemplating the fleeting, ephemeral, and changing nature of the facts gathered by the historian, ethnographer, or analyst of social development, we become aware of the profoundly variable character of human constructions, and also come to know the unsoundness of efforts to make them immutable and lasting.

Between the end of the eighteenth and the middle of the nineteenth centuries, it was common to hear in classrooms, social gatherings, or speeches wherein past events were remembered the saying that: "history is the teacher of life." By this they meant that one who read history books, or examined closely the actions that caused this or that result, could use this knowledge to avoid the mistakes of the past or to lay down rules for one's own life, grounding these in the experiences of the past. As we know, Hegel abruptly ended this pretension with the cutting response: "what experience and history teach us is that peoples and governments have never learned anything from history, and have never acted in accord with the doctrines that they could have drawn from it." In our time, Agnes Heller observed that peoples and governments: "are by no means children, so for them there is no teacher called history."[6]

As Agnes Heller shows, if it is true that we do not draw "lessons from history," we are nonetheless constantly learning historical deeds. Contemporary challenges always send us back to the crossroads of the past, and many times past occurrences serve as the "orienting principles of our present actions." But what all this means is that: "history does not teach us anything," because

> "it is we who, learning from it, learn about ourselves. Historicity, history, is ourselves. We are the teachers and the disciples in this school that is our planet. … History does not 'continue to advance,' because nothing advances in absolute terms. It is we who advance. … Like Vico says, we can only understand the world we ourselves have created. We are not limited to probing in darkness. The beam that illuminates the dark regions of our past is the spotlight of our conscience."[7]

But even when the historian struggles to eliminate or diminish interpretations that distort the past, he is incapable of applying the brakes on the images that stream uninterrupted from the past, or that various actors or social groups produce and invent about the past. Today we know that the peoples and governments of some Latin American, Asian, and European countries while facing in the nineteenth century various threats and opportunities, imagined ties of identity that sought to unite populations of different languages and cultures; invented nonexistent ancestors; produced national symbols (languages, territories, flags, and national anthems); or inaugurated monuments, museums, ceremonies, and heroic pantheons that throughout this century defined the emblems and principles of legitimacy which have guarded the nation and the national state. In this sense, those peoples and governments created "imagined communities" that later challenged the understanding and analyses of historians, sociologists, and political scientists. Standing out among the most effective instruments of the creation of collective identities are the textbook, the map of national territory, the civic calendar, the public ritual and ceremony and the use of the new media of communication.[8]

Another important social function performed by history emerges from the habits established by its very practitioners. In recent centuries, but above all in the one that is now ending, the study of history has become not only a recording of the past, but an analysis of the processes of human development made possible by the critical reconstruction of the past. As Marc Bloch has said: "Real progress came the day that skepticism became 'critical'—as Volney said—; when the objective rules, to put it in other words, worked out little by little the way of choosing between truth and lies."[9]

Through careful examination of the historical record, submitting testimony to rigorous tests of veracity and authenticity, and attending more to the how and why things happened the way they did, historical account has become a critical knowledge, a positive understanding of human experience. Historical inquiry has imposed the rule that "an affirmation cannot be made if it cannot be proven," and warned that "of all the poisons capable of corrupting testimony, falsification is the most violent."

In so far as the historian has exercised greater caution in critiquing and selecting his sources, improved his analytical methods, and acquired the techniques of the exact sciences and of the humanities, he has become the challenger of concepts of historical development based in myths, religion, providential heroes, nationalisms, and ideologies of any bent. In this manner, rather than looking for a transcendental value in human action, of legitimizing power or putting itself at the service of ideologies, the practice of history has become a critical exercise and demystifier as part of a "rational task of analysis" as Marc Bloch has put it.[10]

Pressured by these demands, historical investigation has abandoned universalist interpretations of human development and dedicated itself to studying the actions of individual and collective actors in concrete form, seeking to explain human conduct according to its own logic, and trying to understand historical change through its own developments and as human processes capable of being observed with the analytical tools created by intelligence and empirical knowledge.

It can thus be said that the social function imposed on historical inquiry in our day is to make its practice a rational, critical, intelligent, and comprehensive exercise. That is to say, it has been turned into an empirical study, submitted to the rules of proof and error proper to scientific understanding.

Yet even while historians of this century sometimes dreamed of putting historical understanding on the same level as science, after unfortunate experiences many wound up recognizing that the role of history is not to produce knowledge capable of being proven or refuted through empirical scientific procedure. For unlike the scientist, the historian, as well as the ethnographer or the sociologist, knows that it is not possible to hermetically isolate the object of his study because human actions are intrinsically linked to the social cohort that shapes it. And unlike the positivist historian, who thought he could understand events as they effectively happened in the past, the present historian has accepted the idea that objectivity is an interactive relationship between the inquiry of the investigator and the object that he studies: "The validity of this definition arises more from persuasion than from evidence; but without evidence there is no historical account worthy of the name."[11]

Aside from the differences in focus and practice that now divide historians and the schools of historiography, there is a consensus that the main objective of history is the production of understanding by exercising reasoned explanation.

In spite of the pressures and all that experimental sciences have brought to bear on the field of history, the members of this profession have decided not to close the door on experiences that come from art, the humanities, and common sense. After the lengthy and sometimes heated debates about the scientific methods that lead to true knowledge, the teachers of the profession have proposed to practice with rigor some basic rules. The following ones stand out among them:

Ignore those who want to confine history within a rigid straight jacket of determinism, be it Marxist, structuralist, or functionalist. Avoid falling into monocausal explanations. Keep a distance from the banalities of the antiquarian who invests his time in the past for the sole reason that the facts which repose there are covered by the dust of time. Reject the academic pigeonholes that have divided history into fields, areas, disciplines, and specializations that fragment the understanding of social development.

Tie the history of material life, social history, and cultural history to political history, the analysis of deep structures of power and one of the fields of understanding most neglected in recent decades. Restore the lives of human beings, be they great or small, to the history they were expelled from by the *isms* imposed throughout this century.

Impose, as an essential norm of communication, clarity of language and expression. Fight the tendency that seeks to divide us into groups progressively smaller, more specialized, and isolated. Restore, in the end, the central function of history which is to explain social development.[12] Perhaps this can thus be reduced to showing that with the force of reliable facts and reasoned explanation, historical analysis generates positive knowledge that helps us to understand the behavior, ideas, and legacies of human beings.

Notes

1. See Enrique Florescano, *Memoria mexicana*, (México, 1994). There is also an English edition: *Memory, Myth and Time in Mexico* (Texas University Press, 1993).
2. John Updike, "El escritor como conferenciante," *La Jornada Semanal*, 19 February 1989.
3. Cited by Erwin Panofsky, *El significafo en las artes visuales*, (Madrid, 1991), 38–39.
4. Erik Hornung, *Les dieux de l'Egypte* (Paris, 1992), 233.

5. Agnes Heller, *Teoria de la historia* (Mexico 1989), 165. The preceding reference to Hegel is also drawn from here.

6. Ibid, 179–80.

7. See Josefina Vázquez, *Nacionalismo y educación en México* (México, 1970); David A. Brading, *Los orígenes del nacionalismo mexicano* (México, Secretaría de Educación Pública, 1972); Benedict Anderson, *Imagined Communities* (London, 1991); E.J. Hobsbawm, *Nations and Nationalism since 1780* (London, 1990).

8. Bloch, *Introducción al estudio de la historia* (Mexico, 1952), 166.

9. Ibid, 16.

10. Joyce Appleby, Lynn Hunt and Margaret Jacob, *Telling the Truth about History* (New York, 1994), 260–61.

11. Lawrence Stone, "Una doble función. Las tareas en que se deben empeñar los historiadores en el futuro." *El País*. 29 July, 1993.

The Historian between the Quest for the Universal and the Quest for Identity

E.J. Hobsbawm

It might be best to begin this discussion of the historian's predicament with a concrete experience. In the early summer of 1944, as the German army retreated northwards in Italy to establish a more defensible front against the advancing Allied forces along the so-called "Gothic Line" in the Appenines, its units carried out a number of massacres, usually justified as reprisals against local "bandit" (i.e., partisan) activity. Fifty years later some of these village massacres in the province of Arezzo, hitherto left to the memories of the villages' own survivors and the local historians of the Resistance, provided the occasion for an international conference on the memory of German massacres in World War II.

The conference gathered together not only historians and social scientists from various countries in Eastern and Western Europe and the U.S.A, but local survivors, old resisters, and other interested parties. No subject could be less purely "academic," even fifty years after 175 men were separated from their women and children in Civitella della Chiana, shot and dumped in the burning houses of their village. Hence, not surprisingly, the conference took place in an extraordinary atmosphere of tension and uneasiness. Everyone was aware that matters of major political, even existential, urgency were at stake. Every historian present could not fail to "s'interroge(r) sur sa mission et ses responsabilités vis-à-vis des exigences du temps présent." After all, only a few weeks earlier Italy had elected the first government since 1943 to include Fascists, and was dedicated both to anti-communism and to the proposition that the Resistance of 1943–45 had not been a movement of national liberation and, in any case, that it belonged to a remote past which was irrelevant to the present and ought to be forgotten.

Everyone was uneasy. The survivors of the times of resistance and massacre were uneasy at the bringing into the open of things which, as every countryman and countrywoman knew, were best left unspoken. How, but by a tacit agreement to bury the conflicts of the past, could rural life have returned to any kind of "normality" after 1945? (An American historian produced a perceptive paper about this mechanism of selective silence in his Croatian wife's Istrian village.) The old partisans, and indeed public opinion in the deeply left-wing region of Tuscany, were uneasy at living through a moment when the Italian republic officially rejected the tradition of the Resistance against Hitler and Mussolini, which they (rightly) regarded as its foundation. The young, and presumably mainly left-wing, oral historians who had interviewed or re-interviewed the villagers in preparation for the conference, were shocked to find that, at least in one strongly Catholic village, the inhabitants blamed not so much the Germans for the massacre, but rather the local youngsters who had joined the partisans and, they felt, had irresponsibly plunged their homes into disaster.

Other historians had their own reasons for unease. The German historians present were palpably haunted by what their fathers or grandfathers in 1944 had done, or failed to do. Virtually all non-Italian historians, and several Italian ones, had never heard of the massacres in whose memory the conference was organized: a troubling reminder of the sheer arbitrariness of historical survival and memory. Why had some experiences become part of a wider historical memory, but so many others not? The Russian participants made no secret of their belief that a concentration of scholarship on Nazi atrocities was a means of diverting attention from the horrors of Stalinism. The specialists in the history of World War II, irrespective of their national backgrounds, could not avoid the question, fifty years after the event, of whether the massacres of the innocent that spring—amounting it was said, to over 1% of the total population of the province of Arezzo—were a justifiable price to pay for the relatively minor military harassment of a German force which was in any case planning to withdraw from the area within a matter of days or, at most, weeks.

The very subject matter of the conference, atrocity, was impossible to contemplate dispassionately. Rightly, attention was not confined to local micro-history, but broadened out to consider the greater atrocities of genocide, some of whose leading historians were also present, and the wider problem of how such things are, or can be, remembered. Yet as we stood on the rebuilt piazza of a once destroyed village, listening to the elaborate commemorative narrative which the survivors and the children of the dead had constructed about that terrible day in 1944, how could we fail to see that our kind of history was not merely incompatible with theirs, but in some ways destructive of it? What was the nature of the communication between the historian, who presented the mayor of the village with the transcript of the enquiry into the massacre made by the British army a few days after it had occurred, and the mayor who received it? For one it was a primary archival source, for the other a reinforcement of the village's memorial discourse, which we historians easily recognized as partly mythological. Yet that memorial narrative was a way of coming to terms with a trauma which was as profound for Civitella della Chiana as the holocaust is for the totality of the Jewish people. Was our history, designed for the universal communication of what could be tested by evidence and logic, relevant to their memorial, which, by its nature, belonged to no one but themselves? Which, as we learned, the villagers had for decades kept to themselves for this reason, refusing, out of a tact which we did not share, to enquire into the details of a neighboring village massacre because that was not their past but their neighbors'? Was our history comparable to theirs at all?

In short, no occasion could have better dramatized the confrontation between universality and identity in history, and the historians' confrontation with both past and present.

Nevertheless, this very confrontation demonstrated that for historians universality necessarily prevailed over identity. As it happened at least one historian present represented both in his own person. The organizer of the conference had himself stood on the piazza of Civitella as a small child with his mother as the Germans dragged away and slaughtered his father. He was still part of the village, where he spent the summer in the old family house. Nobody could possibly deny that for him, as for all his followers, the massacre held memories and meanings which it could not hold for the rest of us, or that he would read even the archival records differently from any researcher who did not share his experience.

And yet, as a historian he confronted the memorial narrative which the village had constructed for itself in exactly the same way as the historians lacking this personal involvement, namely by applying the rules and criteria of our discipline. By his and our standards—by the universally accepted criteria of the discipline— the village narrative had to be tested against the sources, and by these standards it was not history, although the formation of this village memory, its institutionalization, and its changes over the past fifty years were part of history. It was itself a subject for historical research by the same methods as the events of June 1944 with which it had tried to come to terms. Only in this respect was the "culture of [Civitella's] identity" relevant to the historians' history of the massacre. In every other respect it was irrelevant.

In short, on the questions with which historical research and theoretical reaction can deal, there was and could be no difference in substance between scholars for whom the identity problems of Civitella were insignificant or uninteresting and an historian for whom they were existentially central. All historians present hoped to agree about the formulation of the questions about the Nazi atrocities, though one would not necessarily expect them to agree about them. All agreed about the procedures for answering these questions, the nature of the possible evidence which would allow them to be answered—insofar as the answers depended on evidence—and about the comparability of events which were experienced by the participants as unique and communicable. Conversely, those who were unwilling to submit their, or their community's, experience to these procedures, or who refused to accept the results of such tests, were outside the discipline of history, however much historians respected their motives and feelings. In fact, among the historians present there was an impressive consensus on matters of substance. It contrasted strikingly with the chaos of varied and conflicting emotions which agitated the participants.

II

The problem for professional historians is that their subject has important social and political functions. These depend on their work—(who else discovers and records the past but historians?), - but at the same time they are at odds with their professional standards. This duality is at the core of our subject. The founders of the *Revue Historique* were conscious of it when they stated, in the *avant-propos* to their first number that "l'étude du passé de la France, qui sera la principale partie de notre tâche, a d'ailleurs aujourd'hui une importance nationale. C'est par elle que nous pouvons rendre à notre pays l'unité et la force morales dont il a besoin."[1]

Of course, nothing was further from their confident, positivist, minds than serving their nation otherwise than by the search for truth. And yet the non-academics who need and use the commodity which historians produce, and who constitute the largest and politically decisive market for it, are untroubled by the sharp distinction between the "procédés strictement scientifiques" and the "developpements oratoires," which was so central to the founders of the *Revue*. Their criterion of what is "good history" is "history that is good for us"—"our country," "our cause," or simply "our emotional satisfaction." Whether they like it or not, professional historians produce the raw material for the non-professionals' use or misuse.

That history is inextricably bound to contemporary politics—as the historiography of the French Revolution continues to prove—is probably today not a major difficulty, for the debates of historians, at least in countries of intellectual freedom, are conducted within the rules of the discipline. Besides, many of the most ideologically charged debates among professional historians concern matters about which non-historians know little and care less. However, all human beings, collectivities, and institutions need a past, but it is only occasionally the past uncovered by historical research. The standard example of an identity culture which anchors itself to the past by means of myths dressed up as history is nationalism. Of this Ernest Renan observed more than a century ago, "L'oubli, et je dirai même l'erreur historique, sont un facteur essentiel de la formation d'une nation, et c'est ainsi que le progrès des études historiques est souvent pour la nationalité un danger." For nations are historically novel entities pretending to have existed for a very long time. Inevitably the nationalist version of their history consists of anachronism, omission, de-contextualization and, in extreme cases, lies. To a lesser extent this is true of all forms of identity history, old or new.

In the pre-academic past there was little to prevent pure historical invention, such as the forgery of historical manuscripts (as in Bohemia), the writing of an ancient, and suitably glorious Scottish national epic (like James Macpherson's "Ossian "), or the production of an entirely invented piece of public theater purporting to represent the ancient Bardic rituals, as in Wales. (This still forms the climax of the annual National Eisteddfod or cultural festival of that small country.) Where such inventions have to be submitted to the tests of a large and established scholarly community, this is no longer possible. Much of early historical scholarship consisted of the disproof of such inventions and the deconstruction of the myths built on them. The great English medievalist J. Horace Round made his reputation by a series of merciless dissections of the pedigrees of British noble families whose claim to descent from Norman invaders he showed to be spurious. The tests are not necessarily only historic. The "Turin shroud," to name a recent example of a holy relic of the kind that made the fortunes of medieval pilgrimage centers, could not resist the test of carbon-B dating to which it had to be submitted.

History as fiction has, however, received an academic reinforcement from an unexpected quarter: the "growing skepticism concerning the Enlightenment project of rationality."[2] The fashion for what (at least in Anglo-Saxon academic discourse) is known by the vague term "postmodernism," has fortunately not gained as much ground among historians as among literary and cultural theorists and social anthropologists, even in the U.S.A., but it is relevant to the question at issue, as it throws doubt on the distinction between fact and fiction, objective reality and conceptual discourse. It is profoundly relativist. If there is no clear distinction between what is true and what I feel to be true, then my own construction of reality is as good as yours or anyone else's, for "discourse is the maker of this world, not the mirror."[3] To cite the same author, the object of ethnography, as presumably of any other social and historical enquiry, is to produce a cooperatively evolved text, in which neither subject nor author nor reader, nor indeed anyone, has the exclusive right of "synoptic transcendence."[4] If, "in historical as in literary discourse, even presumably descriptive language *constitutes* what it describes" (M.P.

Smith, *loc cit*, 499), then no narrative among the many possible ones can be regarded as privileged. It is not fortuitous that these views have appealed particularly to those who see themselves as representing collectivities or milieux marginalized by the hegemonic culture of some group (say, middle-class white heterosexual males of Western education) whose claim to superiority they contest. But it is wrong.

Without entering the theoretical debate on these matters, it is essential for historians to defend the foundation of their discipline: the supremacy of evidence. If their texts are fictions, as in some sense they are, being literary compositions, the raw material of these fictions is verifiable fact. Whether the Nazi gas ovens existed or not, can be established by evidence. Because it has been so established, those who deny their existence are not writing history, whatever their narrative techniques. If a novel were to be about the return of the living Napoleon from Saint Helena, it might be literature but could not be history. If history is an imaginative art, it is one which does not invent but arranges objets trouvés. The distinction may appear pedantic and trivial to the non-historian, especially the one who uses historical material for his or her own purposes. What does it matter to the theatrical audience that there is no historical record of a Lady Macbeth urging her husband to kill King Duncan, or of witches predicting that Macbeth would be of Scotland, which indeed he became in 1040–57? What did it matter to the (Pan-African) founding fathers of West African post-colonial states that they gave their countries the names of medieval African empires which had no obvious connection with the territories of the modern Ghana or Mali? Was it not more important to remind sub-Saharan Africans, after generations of colonialism, that they had a tradition of independent and powerful states somewhere on their continent, if not precisely in the hinterland of Accra?

Indeed, the historians' insistence, once again in the words of the first issue of the *Revue Historique*, on "des procédées d'exposition strictement scientifique, ou chaque affirmation soit accompagnée de preuves, de renvois aux sources et de citations,"[5] is sometimes pedantic and trivial, especially now that it no longer forms part of a faith in the possibility of a definitive, positivist scientific truth, which lent it a certain simple-minded grandeur. Yet the procedures of law-court, which insist on the supremacy of evidence as much as historical researchers, and often in much the same manner, demonstrate that the difference between historical fact and falsehood is not ideological. It is crucial for many practical purposes of everyday life, if only because life and death, or—what is quantitatively more important—money, depend on it. When an innocent person is tried for murder, and wishes to prove his or her innocence, what is required is not the techniques of the "postmodern" theorist, but of the old-fashioned historian.

Moreover, the historical verifiability of political or ideological claims can be vitally important, if historicity is the essential basis of such claims. This is true not only of territorial claims by states or communities, which are commonly historic. The anti-Muslim campaign by the integrist Hindu party BJP, which led to large-scale massacre in India, was justified on historic grounds. The city of Ayodhya was claimed to be the birthplace of the divine Rama. For this reason the construction of a mosque on a Hindu holy site, allegedly by the Mogul conqueror Babur, in such a holy place was a Moslem insult to the Hindu religion and an historic outrage. It had to be destroyed and replaced by a Hindu temple. (The mosque was actually torn down by a vast crowd of Hindu zealots, mobilized for this purpose by the BJP.) Not surprisingly, the leaders of that party declared that "such issues cannot be resolved by court verdict," as the historic base of the claim was non-existent. Indian historians were able to show that nobody had regarded Ayodhya as the birthplace of Rama before the nineteenth century and that Mogul emperors had no specific association with the mosque, while legal records showed that the Hindu claim to the site was in dispute. The specific tension between the religious communities was actually recent. It was a time bomb whose fuse had been lit in 1949, when, in the aftermath of the partition of India and the establishment of Pakistan, a "miracle of the images" appearing in the mosque had been fabricated.[6]

To insist on the supremacy of evidence, and the centrality of the distinction between verifiable historical fact and fiction, is only one of the ways of exercising the historian's responsibility, and, as actual historical fabrication is not what it once was, perhaps not the most important. Reading the desires of the present into the past, or, in technical terms, anachronism, is the most common and convenient technique of creating a history satisfying the needs of what Benedict Anderson has called "imagined communities" or collectives, which are by no means only national ones.[7]

The deconstruction of political or social myths dressed up as history, has long been part of the historian's professional duties, independent of his or her sympathies. British historians are, one hopes, as committed to British liberty as anyone, but that does not prevent them from criticizing its mythology. Every British child was once taught at school that the Magna Carta was the foundation of British liberties, but since McKechnie's monograph of 1914 every university student of British history has had to learn that the document extorted from King John by the barons in 1215 was not intended to be a declaration of parliament supremacy and equal rights for freeborn Englishmen, even though it came to be regarded as such in British political rhetoric much later. The skeptical critique of historical anachronism is probably today the chief way in which historians can demonstrate their public responsibility. Their most important public role today, especially in the numerous states founded or reconstituted since World War II, is to practice his craft in such a way as to constitute "pour la nationalite" (and for all other ideologies of collective identity) "un danger."

This is dramatically obvious in situations in which international conflicts hinge on historical argument, as over the present phase of the always explosive Macedonian question. Everything about this incendiary issue, which involves four countries and the European Union and may once again launch a Balkan war, is historical. The ostensible history brandished by the chief contending parties is ancient, for both Macedonia and Greece (which refuses any other independent state even the use of the name) claim the heritage of Alexander the Great. The real history is relatively contemporary, for the actual dispute between Greece and its neighbors arises out of the division of Macedonia after the Balkan Wars of 1912 between Greece, Serbia, and Bulgaria. All of it had previously been part of the Ottoman Empire. The Greeks ended up with the greater part of it. Which of the successor states has a claim to what part of the undefined but large territory of pre-1913

Macedonia (for the Ottoman Empire did not use the name) has always been argued in terms of academic scholarship, mostly ethnographic and linguistic. The Greek case, which is at present the most vocal, rests largely on anachronistic history because the ethnic and linguistic arguments are more likely to favor Slav and possible Albanian claimants. It is not much more convincing than the argument that France has a claim to Italy because Julius Caesar was the conqueror of Gaul. A historian who points this out is not necessarily moved by prejudice against Greeks or in favor of Slavs, though he or she will at present be more popular in Skopje than in Athens. If the same historian points out that the majority of the population of the greatest city of (undivided) Macedonia, Salonica, was identifiable neither as Greek nor Slav but almost certainly as Moslems and Jews, he or she will be equally unpopular among the nationalist zealots of three countries.

Yet cases such as this also suggest the limitations of the historians' function as destroyer of myth. In the first place, the strength of their critique is negative. A. Popper taught us, that the test of falsification can make a theory untenable, but does not in itself substitute a better one. In the second place, we can demolish a myth only insofar as it rests on propositions which can be shown to be mistaken. It is in the nature of historical myths, especially nationalist ones, that usually only a few of its propositions can be so discredited. The Israeli national ritual constructed round the siege of Masada does not depend on the historically verifiable truth of the patriotic legend learned by Israeli schoolchildren and visiting foreigners, and is therefore not seriously affected by justifiable skepticism of historians specializing in the history of Roman Palestine. Moreover, even where the test can be applied, when evidence is absent, defective, conflicting, or circumstantial it cannot convincingly refute even a highly implausible proposition. Evidence can show conclusively, against those who deny it, that the Nazi genocide of the Jews took place, but, though no serious historian doubts that Hitler wanted the "Final Solution," it cannot demonstrate that he gave a specific order to this effect. Given Hitler's mode of operation, such a specific written order is unlikely, and none has been found. So, whereas it is not difficult to dismiss the theses of M.Faurisson, we cannot, without elaborate argument, reject the case made by David Irving, as most experts in the field do.

The third limitation on the historians' function as myth-slayer is even more obvious. In the short run they are impotent against those who choose to believe historical myth, especially if they hold political power, which, in many countries, and especially the numerous new states, entails control over what is still the most important channel of imparting historical information, the schools. And, let it never be forgotten, history—mainly national history—occupies an important place in all known systems of public education.the Indian historians' critique of the historic myths of Hindu fanaticism may convince their academic colleagues, but not the zealots of the BJP party. The Croatian and Serb historians who resist the imposition of a nationalist legend on the history of their states, have had less influence than the long-distance nationalists of the Croat and Serb diasporas, moved by nationalist mythology immune to historical critique.

III

These limitations do not diminish the public responsibility of the historian. This rests, first and foremost, on the fact, already noted above, that historians as an occupation are the primary producers of the raw material that is turned into propaganda and mythology. We must be aware that this is so, particularly at a time when alternative ways of preserving the past—oral tradition, family memory, everything that depends on the effectiveness of intergenerational communications which are disintegrating in modern societies—are disappearing. In any case the history of large collectivities, national or other, has not rested on popular memory, but on what historians, chroniclers, or antiquarians have written about the past, directly or through school textbooks, on what teachers have taught their pupils from those school books, on how writers of fiction, film producers, or the makers of television and video programs have transformed their material. Even Shakespeare's *Hamlet* was derived at various removes from the work of a historian, the Danish chronicler Saxo Grammaticus. lt is quite essential that historians should constantly remember this. The crops we cultivate in our fields may end up as some version of the opium of the people.

It is true, of course, that the inseparability of historiography from current ideology and politics—all history, as Croce said, is contemporary history—opens the way to the misuse of history. Historians do not and cannot stand outside their subject as objective observers and analysts *sub specie aeternitatis*. All of us are plunged into the assumptions of our times and places, even when we practice something as far removed from today's public passions as the editing of old texts. Many of us, like the founder of the *Revue Historique*, are happy to produce work that can be of use to our people or cause. We will no doubt be tempted to interpret our findings in the way most favorable to the cause. We may be tempted to abstain from enquiring into topics likely to throw unfavorable light on it. It is not surprising that historians hostile to communism were considerably more likely to research into forced labor in the USSR than historians sympathetic to it. We may even be tempted to remain silent about unfavorable evidence, if we happen to discover it, though hardly with a good scholarly conscience. After all, no sharp line divides *suppressio veri* from *suggestio falsi*. What we cannot do without ceasing to be historians is to abandon the criteria of our profession. We cannot say what we can show to be untrue. In this we inevitably differ from those whose discourse is not so constrained.

Yet the major danger lies, not in the temptation to lie, which, after all, cannot easily survive the scrutiny of other historians in a free scholarly community, though political pressure and authority provide a buttress for untruth, even in some constitutional states. It lies in the temptation to isolate the history of one part of humanity—the historian's own, by birth or choice—from its wider context.

The internal and external pressures to do so may be great. Our passions and interests may urge us in this direction. Every Jew, for instance, whatever his or her occupation, instinctively accepts the force of the question with which, during many threatening centuries, members of our minority community, confronted any and every event in the wider world: "Is it good for the Jews? Is it bad for the Jews?" In times of discrimination or persecution it provided guidance—though not necessarily the best guidance—for private and public behavior, a strategy at all levels for a scattered people. Yet it cannot and should not guide a Jewish historian, even one who writes the history of his own people. Historians, however microcosmic, must be for universalism, not out of loyalty to an ideal to which many of us remain attached but because it is the necessary condition for understanding the history of humanity, including that of any special section of humanity. For all human collectivities necessarily are and have been part of a larger and more complex world. A history which is designed *only* for Jews (or African-Americans, or Greeks, or women, or proletarians, or homosexuals) cannot be good history, though it may be comforting history to those who practice it.

Unfortunately, as the situation in large parts of the world at the end of our millennium demonstrates, bad history is not harmless history. It is dangerous. The sentences typed on apparently innocuous keyboards may be sentences of death.

Notes

1. G. Monod and G. Fagniez, "Avant-propos," in *Revue Historique*, I, 1 (1876), 4.
2. Michael Smith, "Postmodernism,urban ethnography, and the new social space of ethnic identity" in *Theory and Society*, 21 (August, 1992), 493.
3. Stephen A. Tyler, *The Unspeakable* (Madison, 1987), 171.
4. Stephen A. Tyler, "Post-Modern Ethnography: From Document of the Occult to Occult Document" in James Clifford and George Marcus, eds., *Writing Culture, The Poetics and Politics of Ethnography* (1986), 126, 129.
5. G. Monod and G. Fagniez, "Avant-propos," 2.
6. Romila Thapar, "The Politics of Religious Communities"in *Seminar 365*, (January, 1990), 27–32.
7. Benedict Anderson, *Imagined Communities. Reflections on the Origin and Spread of Nationalism* (Revised edition, London, 1991).

The Double Responsibility
of the Historian

Aaron I. Gurevich

I am an historian in a country in which it is not only impossible to say what the future will be, but in which the past itself—as someone put it—is susceptible to change. This country is currently going through an unprecedented crisis that has turned both its material and political as well as spiritual life upside-down. The crisis, the roots of which stretch back over decades, has made life virtually unbearable for many of its citizens. Yet for the historian, and for the philosopher and sociologist, this crisis affords an unusual opportunity. As a result of the earthquakes that have shaken the former Soviet Union, formerly hidden layers of history—and the forces that underpin them—have been revealed. Such cases do not often arise. To a scholar endeavoring to discover the secret springs of unfolding events, Russia represents a gigantic and unique "laboratory." Although it is easier to judge the extent of a cataclysm, to comprehend its deeper import, after the event, this does not relieve the contemporary—who participates in historical events—of the duty of trying to understand, to the extent possible, the nature of the changes taking place.

Our society, so long caught in the iron grip of an implacable ideology, had no conception of the emotions and spiritual conditions that exist side by side with ideas and official dogma, state plans and governmental laws; that in the depths of human conscience there exists a world-view that determines individual and collective behavior. Mentalities, non-official value systems, personal convictions were ignored; their existence was even denied and veiled by the façade of the *apparat*. In this way a misleading image of the people and the State was generated; in this way were formed the false notions of the ideologues, and the historians among them, concerning the nature of the historical process. And so it happened that all the magma hidden in the depths of history suddenly erupted and became visible in broad daylight, catching the politicians, historians, and scholars unaware. Simultaneously Marxist historiosophy, which had previously subjugated historical thinking, lost all credibility, leaving behind a philosophical void that was filled with whatever was available; from mysticism and occultism to an aggressive chauvinism. This combination of a manipulated historical memory and the nostalgia resulting from the collapse of the Soviet empire caused the picture of the past to undergo the most unexpected and arbitrary reconstructions. Superficially and abusively understood, freedom of thought was transformed into irresponsible indulgence. New myths were created from the bones of old ones—myths that at bottom disguised collective inferiority complexes and a wounded imperialism.

Today's challenge is to create a democratic society capable of participating in our global civilization. However, neither politicians nor historians should lose sight of the particularities and socio-psychological background that has dominated Russian history in the past and that is still present, invisible but powerful, in the consciousness of contemporary generations. Only one hundred thirty years ago Russia was still a country of general serfdom and despotism; the fundamental values of a civil society, such as private property, the rule of law, individual liberties, and respect for the human person were either totally absent or existed very much on the margins of social conscience. We must also remember that soon after the Revolution of October 1917 servitude reappeared in the form of collectivization and the Gulag. As for parliamentary government: it must be recognized that its meaning and role are scarcely comprehensible to the members of parliament themselves and that there is a frequent tendency to confuse parliament with the *veche* of ancient Russia or with the assembly of the members of the Communist Party of the Soviet Union that almost all of today's parliamentarians participated in a mere three years ago. As Fernand Braudel put it: "Mentalities are the prisons in which the *longue durée* is locked up;" they change extraordinarily slowly. To introduce democracy and parliamentarianism into a country that is ignorant of them is something of a utopian project.

All these circumstances have created new problems for public officials and politicians, which they are in no way prepared to solve. However, this does not mean that the demagogues who deny the possibility of Russia developing according to the democratic model are right. It must simply be understood that enormous difficulties lie ahead and that we must be dedicated to overcoming them.

Can historians who work under conditions that imply a clean break with the Soviet past continue to adhere to positions whose criteria, methodology, and values were inherited from the now-discredited Communist era? Russian society today finds itself at a crossroads. Disoriented, its values shaken, Russia needs new thinkers and new historians. Are we then prepared, if not to solve the new problems, at least to formulate them, albeit in a "preliminary" form? Before seeking an answer to this question, let us take a look at the relatively recent past.

The Historians' Empty Drawer

In the mid-1980s, with the advent of *glasnost* (a period of relative freedom of expression), important literary journals began to publish the works of Russian poets, writers, and philosophers that until then had been forbidden or were totally unknown (in the best cases they had been published abroad and smuggled into Russia). Readers were immediately struck by the spiritual and artistic wealth that had been hidden from them for decades. During the entire period following the October Revolution, Russian literature had lived on. Authors such as Osip Mandelstam, Boris Pasternak, Anna Akhmatova, Mikhail Bulgakov, Vasily Grossman, Alexander Solzhenitzyn and others had never ceased writing. Moreover, in spite of the Stalinist terror and the obscurantism of the stagnant Brezhnev years, they had made no ideological compromises. The pulse of this clandestine intellectual life had never stopped beating.

On the historians' side, it would have been reasonable to expect the publication of formerly-hidden manuscripts on which historians had worked during the decades of reaction. Yet nothing of the kind occurred. The drawers of the historians were empty. At the end of the 1980s and beginning of the 1990s nothing, or almost nothing, emerged to enrich the historical sciences in Russia, except for the publication of archival documents and various works designed to fill in the "gaps" of the history of Soviet Russia. A rare exception to this was the research done by the eminent specialist of Russian history, Alexander Zimin. In several of his monographs Zimin courageously—given the conditions of the period—suggested a new way of viewing a whole range of problems associated with fifteenth and sixteenth century Russian history. He was the first to raise the question of whether there existed a possible alternative to Russia's actual historical development; that is, whether the political unification of the country could have been centered not in Moscow but in some other center of princely power. His works have only recently been published, ten years after his death. However, and once again, the case of Zimin is practically unique.

Although *perestroika* allowed for the introduction of new materials and freed historians from the obligation of referring at every turn and without relevance to the opinions of the "classics of Marxism-Leninism," Russian historians in fact continued to adhere to previous methodological assumptions. In the new socio-political and ideological atmosphere, Russian historical writing did not make any qualitative progress. It was unable to benefit from the freedom it had been granted. What is the source of the scholarly timidity and theoretical impoverishment of the majority of historians?

The Historians of the 1960s

Let us now go back in time some three decades, to the intellectual and moral awakening of the late 1950s and decade of the 1960s. This awakening was in part a result of the lively methodological debates that followed the denunciation of the (Stalinist) "cult of the personality" at the XXth Congress of the Communist Party of the Soviet Union. One cannot overestimate the liberating and stimulating effect that these debates had on intellectual life. The dogmatism of the Stalinist period was finally, in large measure, abandoned or at least called into question. New hypotheses and scholarly ideas were being advanced. Without doubt, the historians of the 1960s did much to prepare the ground for a freer analysis of the historical process. But the "thaw" did not last long, and in the second half of the 1960s, notably after the Soviet invasion of Czechoslovakia, there occurred a new and durable ideological "freeze." To be sure, not all the gains of the beginning of the 1960s were lost, but generally speaking historical writing lapsed into lethargy.

Furthermore, the historians of the 1960s did not, in my view, address the central methodological questions. In fact, as I review today the debates of the past thirty years, I realize how one-sided and narrow they were. This was, of course, inevitable and understandable. Although rejecting or calling into question many of the broad generalizations of the Russian Marxist Vulgate (whose dominant theme was the "new and more profound reading of Marx"), the historians of the 1960s did not touch upon the latent epistemology of Marxism, which Marx had borrowed from Hegel and that rejected the Kantian problematic and its neo-Kantian formulation. Convinced of the omnipotence of scientific knowledge, the Marxists were not inclined to analyze the limits of the conceptual apparatus they were using. Equally, Hegel's and Marx's panlogism, with its disinterest in the complex relationship between the inquiring subject and the object of knowledge, accorded perfectly with the positivism of Russian Marxist historians. Unfortunately, this doomed Soviet historical thinking to a methodology based on the discoveries of late-nineteenth century science. This lag and stagnation were aggravated by an almost total ignorance of contemporary historical thought beyond Russia's borders. This lack of knowledge created a certain intellectual provincialism that in fact endures to this day.

The danger of remaining aloof from the neo-Kantian theory of knowledge was well understood by eminent Russian historians of an earlier period. At the end of the 1920s, for example, the medievalist Dimitri Petrushevsky underscored, in the introduction to one of his books, the enormous importance of the ideas of Heinrich Rickert and Max Weber for historical research. Unfortunately, the most important result of this courageous demonstration of intellectual independence was his being immediately silenced. His declaration had as much of an effect as a cry in the desert: all subsequently published Soviet works on philosophical and methodological subjects continued to reject and denigrate neo-Kantian thought. Until quite recently no one in Russia had objectively studied the "sciences of culture" that the neo-Kantians had proposed at the beginning of the century. Consequently, the supposed "Marxist historical science" became in the end nothing more than positivism dressed up in Marxist phraseology.

Thus, during *glasnost*, the historians proved to the more timid and ideologically docile than the poets and writers. How is this difference in behavior to be explained? Was it perhaps that the historians, being closer to the centers of power, were easier to control? To be sure, writers had not been free to write whatever they pleased; still, they were not constantly obliged to refer to the "Fathers" of the Marxist church, while the historians could not rid themselves of this ritual. It must however be added that the majority of them in fact needed these ideological "crutches."

The "Ideal Type" and the "Socio-Economic Formation"

During the 1980s an eminent French historian asserted that the ideas of Marx and Lenin were not at all "an intellectual strait jacket" for Soviet historians, but rather useful instructions to help them in their research. There is no doubt that Marxism has deeply influenced contemporary historical scholarship. However, is our honorable French colleague really correct? Marxist historiosophy urged historians to illustrate general historical laws—laws formulated by Marxist historiosophy itself—by forbidding historians to diverge from an all-inclusive framework provided by successive stages of "socio-economic formation." This concept of "formation" was thereby viewed as an objective reality. The convenience of this system lay, among other things, in its extraordinary simplicity. The hypothesis that the material-economic "base" determined the ideological and political "superstructure" offered a kind of practical "master key" for a simplified explanation of a society's spiritual life.

On the other hand, Max Weber's "ideal type" does not pretend to be more than an instrument of knowledge, a scientific model (a "utopian ideal" of research), which the historian can make use of in the study of historical phenomena. This model does not "crush" the concrete evidence to which it is applied. On the contrary, the model itself can be modified and, when necessary, thrown out by the historian if it contradicts the concrete evidence. It is precisely the divergence between the actual data and the "ideal type" that allows for fresh insights and even new generalizations. By stressing the influence of religion and other spiritual structures upon social life and production, the author of *The Protestant Ethic and the Spirit of Capitalism* placed man—the thinking, feeling, and acting being—at the center of historical research. Not politico-economic abstractions but man became the basis of historical analysis.

The contrast between the reified abstraction of the "socio-economic formation" ("means of production") and the "ideal type" is striking and intractable. By submitting to a dogma that was imposed upon them, Soviet historians deprived themselves of their freedom as scientists. For a good number of them this lack of intellectual independence was combined with a palpable cynicism.

For hundreds, if not for thousands of Soviet historians, the "critique of bourgeois historiography" became a means of subsistence. How many of them really believed in the much-vaunted "superiority of Soviet science," and how many were merely cynics and opportunists? God only knows. To give but one example: at the time of the publication in Moscow, in 1973, of Marc Bloch's *Apologie pour l'histoire*, one of the pillars of official Soviet historiography said bluntly: "The translation of *Apologie pour l'histoire* is a political error ..."

How many times did I hear my colleagues complain that they were not allowed to write what they wanted? "Censorship constrains us," they said. This was no doubt true, since government censors and the bureaucrats in charge of ideological surveillance kept a close watch on our writings. However, this reasoning is also an extreme simplification of the actual situation. In reality, the majority of authors of historical works practiced self-censorship, which meant that the works they submitted for publication did not actually risk official disapproval. Moreover, who forced them to publish works that were contrary to their own convictions?

Let us be wary, however, of tarring all Soviet historians with the same brush. They were in fact a very diverse group—the young generation of historians especially needs to understand this. Some years ago, during a seminar I conducted, a young historian, who had analyzed in his paper the methodological premises upon which the works of Soviet historians were based, ended by rejecting them as scientifically inconsistent. To the extent that these premises were extremely narrow and one-sided, he was no doubt right: the less-than-satisfying results produced by this kind of historiography are proof. Indeed little of value remains, it is now largely a corpse. However, the same young man did not take into account that the drama of ideas reflected in their works—ideas that have been so criticized and are today rejected—was also a drama of men, of scholars, who found themselves in an intolerable situation. Under such conditions, Soviet historians could not, except in a few rare cases, fulfill their role as mediators between those who once lived and their own society. This situation was the same for the whole of the socialist camp, except perhaps Poland, which represented a happy exception.

History and Society

At the beginning of my career, historical works addressed two categories of readers: on the one hand, a narrow circle of specialists and, on the other, the censors and controllers of ideology. Between the historian and society there existed no "mutual relationship"—a relationship natural and essential for both sides. This connection had been ruptured, and as a result the discipline of history was both sterile and ineffective. Can today's historian continue to ignore this connection?

Huizinga considered history to be one of the ways by which a society acquires self-knowledge. To this end historians implicitly rely on the concept of "the other," by means of which the men of today can compare themselves to men of the past. In the course of history humanity changes; today's human is not yesterday's; his view of the world and social behavior systems that are influenced by it evolve too. The "other," the man of the distant or recent past, is an enigma that we can hardly "solve," but that we must nevertheless try to elucidate. The historian's greatest sin is when he tries to present men of another period as identical to himself and his contemporaries. However, "other" does not mean "stranger."

This "other" resembles us in many ways; but it is particularly important to render the differences intelligible. "Alterity" is a basic postulate of historical understanding.

There exists a dialogue between us and the people of the past. The questions we ask of men of other cultures and civilizations are questions that preoccupy us, that are related to our own culture: we cannot ask any others. Each era brings with it fresh questions concerning the past, we never cease questioning the people of the past. This is the way that historical knowledge advances. The notion of dialogue is not a metaphor. It must, I believe, be taken literally.

During the 1950s, having learned from my teachers analytic methods applicable to the socio-economic conditions of medieval Germany and England, I decided to apply this same methodology to investigating medieval Scandinavian sources. However, I quickly ran into difficulties. Although I had many and diverse texts before me, they remained mute, gave no answer to the questions I had put to them concerning the exploitation of peasants, the structure of peasant communities, and other topics of this kind that were traditional to a Marxist analysis. My difficulties continued until I finally began to listen to the voices of the people who had actually written the texts and to those for whom the texts had been written. They spoke to me of a different matter: of the representation of a world that was as much related to nature as to social existence, of man's place in the world, of his beliefs, passions, behavior; of the magic of rituals, of imagination, pagan gods and belief in another world. When I finally began to understand the meaning of the messages contained in the sources, I became convinced that my questions concerning material life and social structure had meaning only within the framework of this general context. This lesson, taught to me by the Scandinavians of the Middle Ages, had considerable methodological significance for me.

The Historian—the Only Intermediary Between the Contemporary World and the Past

In order to play this role, the historian must appreciate the deeper intellectual needs of the society to which he belongs. He contributes to the formation of the historical consciousness of his society. This is an enormous responsibility, and it is crucial that he be fully conscious of his mission as a mediator between different cultures. The picture he draws of the past depends on the angle from which he views it. Depending on whether the focus is on social contradictions and class conflicts, upon the links between production and property or, alternatively, upon ways of conceiving of the world and the forms of human behavior (the context of which throws fresh light on the socio-economic structures themselves), the entire picture of the past undergoes modification and the approach to history itself changes. The character and contents of the historical knowledge of a given society are dependent on the ways in which history is conceived and represented by historians under the pressures brought by of outside forces. Until recently history was presented to children in Soviet schools exclusively from the angle of class struggle and revolution, a succession of forms of workers' exploitation. Consequently, spiritual life was relegated to the second rank and man was eliminated as a subject of the historical process. The future teachers themselves, that is, university students, received corresponding instruction. From childhood to adulthood, Soviet man was educated in a spirit of class hatred. Today we can see the fruits of that "education."

Only now do we have the opportunity to rewrite school history books, freed of the dogmatism that killed living history. The ideological struggle has been extended to a struggle over the intellectual development of our children. In other words, the perspective that a society adopts to analyze its past depends on its conception of the present and the idea it has of its future.

However, the question is not limited to the responsibility that the historian has toward his contemporaries. He is equally responsible toward those who have already sunken into the waters of Lethe, toward those who speak to us from the historical sources. There is no return from the past for them. The task of "making them alive" (to use Michelet's expression) has fallen on the historian. The historian alone can engage in this risky operation—by remaining fully conscious of the relativity of his efforts.

A Crisis of Historical Science?

It is indisputable that historical scholarship in Russia is in deep crisis. Still, it must be recognized that this crisis, in one way or another, has also impinged upon historical writing around the world. However, it is my opinion that this crisis is akin to a growing pain. Could it not even be regarded as the normal state of the sciences? In fact, an absence of crisis, controversies, and doubts would be a symptom of stagnation. As Jan Romein put it, "History is perpetual controversy." In his *Apologie pour l'histoire* Marc Bloch emphasized that History as a scientific discipline is still young and still *in situ nascendi*. The problem involves not simply the array of techniques used by the historians, but more importantly the fact that the science of history has freed itself from the millstone of philosophy only relatively recently. The universal systems, be it the providential and symbolic theory of the medieval historians or the systems of Hegel, Marx, Spengler, or Toynbee, were like Procrustean beds on which historians were required to "lay down" their materials. Today, historiosophy, whatever its stripe, has been fundamentally discredited (or at least we may hope so); historical science has ceased being the prisoner of *a priori* teleological and metaphysical constructions. The historians have issued their declaration of independence. To be sure, it would be stupid to deny the considerable role that philosophical theories have played in the historian's intellectual development, since ignorance of philosophy and a helpless eclecticism would only doom the historian to theoretical inconsistency. However, the topic of "the historian and philosophy" is beyond the framework of this article and we cannot examine it here.

Starting with this declaration of independence, history must acquire a new intellectual charter and elaborate its own theory of knowledge. Unlike philosophy, sociology, and political economy, history is a science not of general laws but of the concrete, the individual, the unique and the unrepeatable. Nonetheless, historians use concepts and categories that are furnished by their culture and language. When we use the notions of "society," "civilization," "city," "revolution," "economy," etc., we do not study them in terms of general sociological and economic categories: we study a city in a defined period, a particular civilization, a given and concrete revolution. The emphasis is on the unique and on the unrepeatable. Let me illustrate this hypothesis with an example. For a long time there was a marked tendency among Soviet researchers to compare cultures from different regions in order to call attention to recurrent phenomena that were supposed to reflect universal historical laws. Scholars sought to discover a renaissance in Japan, in Central Asia, in Transcaucasia, and then without further ado they would "assimilate" it to the occidental European Renaissance. From superficial coincidences that in fact veiled fundamental differences, one proceeded to pervert completely the meaning of the concrete historical notion of a "renaissance." Have the historians who sought a ubiquitous feudalism—from Assyria and ancient Babylon to the Roman Empire and Kiev Russia, and even Africa— not committed the same error? Comparatist scholarship can serve ends that are totally opposed to one another. It can bring together phenomena that are totally heterogeneous, and under the pretext of likeness arrive at commonplaces that are devoid of meaning. By contrast, when Marc Bloch compared feudal society in France to the traditional social system of Japan (the two structures indisputably present a certain resemblance), he sought to discover the deeper specificity and uniqueness of the two objects being compared. The comparative method reveals its full efficacy as a working tool when used to bring out divergences and particularities, or to put it differently, when it can demonstrate what is characteristic about an individual historical event.

A Reorientation

After Einstein and Freud the rethinking of the historian's craft and its cognitive foundations has become inevitable. Historians can no longer limit themselves to ideas that have been formulated solely in a rational manner, neglecting emotional and irrational psychic phenomena that are not expressed clearly (however I do remain skeptical concerning the possibility of applying the procedures and concepts of psychoanalysis to the study of the past and notably to the distant past). This questioning of the rational also arises because of the Gulag, Auschwitz, and Hiroshima. The notion of an ascent of humanity has broken down, and the question of "giving meaning to the absurd" (an expression of Theodor Lessing's, used to define historiography) has a different meaning today than it did at the end of the 19th and beginning of the 20th century.

The science of history is slowly liberating itself from the weight of politico-economic and sociological abstractions in order to become what it must become in the modern world: a science of man as a social being. To be sure, history in the past was also a science of man; but the men on whom the historians focused were those of the "first rank" —managers, politicians, military leaders, great thinkers, writers. In other words, the heroes of history were historic personages who had left their mark on the development of history. The mass of society, the anonymous participants in the historical process, formed a kind of impersonal background similar to the choir of an ancient Greek tragedy. Today the inadequacy of these approaches has become more and more clear. Great men do not act in a vacuum; it has become indispensable to take into account the society in which they live—not as a grand abstraction, but as a collection of large and small groups into which those whom we call "ordinary people" are organized. The historian cannot, and in general does not, know their names and biographies; but he cannot ignore that they existed and acted and that their life and activities were organized within a specific framework that was defined by the culture and mentalities of the time. The world-view and forms of behavior of ordinary people left their mark on the actions, ideas, and public statements of great men.

The historian must therefore find new ways of studying his subject; ways that will help him gain an understanding of society's anonymous masses. A fresh reading of the sources is necessary in order to grasp the consciousness and behavior of "ordinary men" in a given period. To use Jacques Le Goff's terminology, the historian should not only be concerned with Caesar's intentions but with the mood of his legionnaires; he should be concerned not only with the plans of Christopher Columbus but with the expectations of the sailors on his ships. One could say the same of Clovis and of Charlemagne. We cannot rely merely on the biographies that

Gregory of Tours and Einhard have left us; we must also analyzes the *leges barbarorum*, the capitularies and cartularies, the archaeological remains, the "Lives" of the saints, the penitentials and other evidence that might help to illuminate the social relations, ways of life, beliefs, and ethical norms of ordinary Francs.

History "from above" is in itself insufficient; it has to be linked to history "from below." Here it is not just a matter of studying solely what has been called "popular culture" (a concept as indispensable as it is imprecise and even ambiguous). We must also make a study of different kinds of consciousness; along with the articulated thoughts of individuals, historians must also learn to penetrate the secrets of mentalities, the latent strata of collective conscience.

Studying History "from the Inside"

An essential stage in the development of the historical sciences will be the adoption of a point of view "from the inside," that is, the exploration of the immanent situation of the participants of the historical process; their relationship to life, their mentalities, and their value systems. Obviously the historian can not avoid applying his own concepts to his objects of study; nor can he avoid developing generalizations from his observations based on contemporary theories of knowledge. Nevertheless, this does not give him the right to ignore the vision of the world of the people whose history he is studying. If he did so the historian would end up depicting them as will-less automatons, subject to the play of abstract socio-economic forces.

At the same time traditional approaches to historical research, such as political history, the history of ideas (*Geistesgeschichte*) or socio-economic analysis, should not be abandoned. However, in the clear light of this new perspective, they must inevitably acquire a different meaning, that is, they will cease being self-contained. In this connection it seems appropriate to me to attach particular importance to the notion of "historical context." When an historian sets himself a problem he delineates a set of questions to study; but, having done so, he must clearly see which vital links have been severed—and will hence lie outside his analytical framework—by this delimitation. On this point we can refer to the example I gave above concerning my own difficulties in dealing with medieval Scandinavian sources. The new questions I had to pose were oriented toward the real value system of those Scandinavians; toward their religious and occult images, toward the importance they attached to gold and silver, which for them reflected not so much forms of economic wealth as the tangible manifestations of the "success" and "luck" of certain people. It was only in this new, broader context that the deeper meaning of these social links were revealed.

In traditional historical writing, culture and society were studied in isolation, as distinct subjects without links or as merely mechanically united within the framework of a "base/superstructure" model. Perhaps the most glaring example of this dichotomy, yet one that brings out the essential unity of history, can be found in scholarly textbooks where the chapters devoted to cultural history are presented as appendices outside the main text. Yet if the historian were to ponder the notion of "culture," and if he were to make use of way it is applied by cultural anthropology (that is, as a way of perceiving and understanding the social and spiritual world: symbolic systems applied to the world through consciousness and reorganized in its own way; forms of behavior—economic, political, religious, artistic—that are determined by those systems), the historian's approach would inevitably change, and he would perceive the internal connections between the cultural and social aspects of human activity. Culture and society are two sides of the same coin; it is the historian's thought that opposes them. In fact, culture and society are inherently an indissoluble whole. This is why the development, within the framework of traditional historiography, of historical anthropology (the more cumbersome term of socio-cultural anthropology would be more appropriate)—a field that has clearly taken shape during the past two or three decades and that is known as the "New History"—is perfectly legitimate and even essential.

History in the Anthropological Vein

Historical anthropology does not aspire to replace the other genres of historical research; rather it offers a novel and larger context within which the past can be studied. By its nature historical anthropology adds a new dimension to our vision of history—a dimension without which history will lose its vigor and probing force. Historical anthropology focuses on the study of images of the world, semiotic systems, and basic aspects of human behavior that are latent and therefore without explicit expression. It is based on the idea that all historical existence is the concrete expression of the languages of culture that have created it; to decipher this language requires a penetration of the deeper layers of consciousness, both of the author of the document and of his and or her milieu. [1]

The historical document is therefore not a well from which the historian can freely draw facts; nor is it an open window to the past through which one merely has to look in order to see the past "as it really was." The first task of the historian is to endeavor to understand the language of the period under study (language in the semiotic sense of the term) in an attempt to discover its specific meaning. At the same time the historian cannot shirk another task; he must subject his own analytical instruments to constant analysis, since these instruments carry contemporary meanings and therefore run the risk of deforming the picture of the past.

The nexus of scholar and the past is exceptionally contradictory. The historian studies history through an extremely complex, deforming prism. This prism absorbs the rays that the scholar is emitting at the same time as it incorporates the signals sent by people of the past. The historian then synthesizes them, each time in a new way. In other words the historian, using the historical sources, applies his own conceptual framework to the information to be analyzed. This framework is based on contemporary standards of the human sciences, which themselves reflect the intellectual norms of the society at large. Ought we not then conclude from this that the historian's encounter with the period under study occurs in a temporal locus which is as distinct from the present as it is from the past? It is a unique temporal locus created by the historian.

It seems to me that all these considerations imply the necessity of elaborating an epistemology specific to history. In contrast to historiosophy, which is now discredited, the specific epistemology of history suggested here need not create a single univer-sally-applicable framework. Instead of a single system applied from without to the infinitely varied materials of history, we sug-gest an *ad hoc* hermeneutical method that will develop within the process of research itself. This method should be based both on the particular historical sources being studied and the analytic methods being used.

Toward a New Synthesis

Numerous critics of the new trends in historical writing, notably those of the "New History," have spoken of the destruction of the generalized picture of the past. What we get instead, they say, is unconnected bits and pieces. Is this criticism justified? If what we get instead of an overall picture of the historical process is a mere description of disparate aspects of mentalities, considered inde-pendently of the analysis of social structures, then this criticism is well-founded. On the other hand, if these socio-psychological aspects of history can be integrated into an overall socio-cultural system, then they can be seen as component parts of an histori-cally concrete whole. In this case we are not then witnessing the "collapse" (or "explosion") of the science of history but rather a search for fresh approaches to historical synthesis; and synthesis is the only direction in which history can tend today. The study of particular mentalities is merely the means by which our under-standing of man's nature—as it was during a certain period of his-tory, shaped by the culture and the society of his time—is deepened. Actual historical man: this is the central concern of socio-cultural anthropology as it relates to history; mentalities are no more than the particular episodes in this process.

The Ideal Historian of the 21st Century

I have tried to differentiate between the two aspects of the problem of the "responsibility of the historian": his responsibility toward the society to which he belongs, and his responsibility toward the people of the past whose history he is studying. However, to separate them and to examine them individually is difficult if not impossible, since they overlap. The historian's equitability as far as his own epoch is concerned simultaneously requires that he be equitable toward people whom he tries "to bring back to life." Obviously, since we are talking about a "rebirth" of generations that have disappeared, we can not allow ourselves to be carried away by the Romantic fantasies of Michelet's age; nor should we attempt to "live," "to feel" the psychology of the people of the past, as Dilthey would have it. This kind of endeavor is too subjective. What concerns us here is the development of verifiable research procedures that will provide the historian with the necessary material to reconstruct in a scholarly fashion the world-view, value systems and forms of social behavior of men of a given period.

The model historian of the end of the 20th and beginning of the 21st century (a kind of ideal, a desideratum) appears before my eye as a scholar who ponders the past maturely and attentively, while always continuing to perfect his own cognitive instruments. He constantly reevaluates his thoughts and never forgets to examine critically the premises from which he started, his analytical methods and the kinds of generalizations with which he works. This is neither Ranke's "grand eye-witness," nor the grim positivist slave to historical texts (let us remember the eccentric scholars described by Anatole France), nor the undiscerning collectors of all available and imaginable facts. Rather he is a thinker who compares his own world-view, as well as the world-view of his own milieu, with the world-view of the people whom he is studying.

This historian has irrevocably rid himself of the illusion that the progress achieved through science moves it ever closer to a truth that has remained immutable through the ages. He understands clearly that scientific truth, which generalizes the attainments of contemporary knowledge, is conditioned by the questions that preoccupy our society; for this reason it is historically concrete and will be revised simultaneously and proportionately to the evolution of socio-cultural circumstances. He is open to the dialogue between cultures; indeed the social significance of his work is a result of this dialogue. The discipline of history, so constituted, is better prepared to resist the emergence of false new historical mythologies that try to transform history into a servant of politics, of a dominant ideology or of vulgar prejudices circulating among the public—all of which can only shake the confidence in a discipline in which we must believe.

Notes

1. See A. I. Gurevich, "History and Historical Anthropology," in: Diogenes 151, 79–94.

History and the Public Use of History

Nicola Gallerano

I intend to explore the relationship between the history of historians and the public use of history. This relationship, in my opinion, is both conflictual and convergent. As we shall see later on, this assertion is anything but obvious; among historians the idea of a neat opposition prevails, with no possibility of reconciliation, between professional practices of history (the profession of historians) and the extremely vast and confused domain of its "public use."[1]

Before undertaking an analysis, I must explain what I mean by the public use of history. I have adopted, at least initially, a purely extrinsic definition of the term. By the "public use of history" I am referring to all that is developed outside the domain of scientific research in its strictest sense, outside the history of historians which is usually written by scholars and intended for a very limited segment of the population. Public use of history includes not only the various means of mass communication, each with its own particularities (journalism, radio, television, cinema, theater, photography, advertisement, etc.), but also the arts and literature; public places such as schools, history museums, monuments and urban spaces, etc., and finally institutions, formal or otherwise (such as cultural associations, parties, and religious, ethnic and cultural groups, etc.), which, with more or less clearly partisan objectives, endeavor to promote a more or less polemic reading of the past as compared to the generally accepted common sense of history or historiography, a polemical reading based on the memory of their respective groups. Indeed, politicians have a large role in the most visible and most talked about manifestations of the public use of history and they have a particular responsibility in its degeneration (I shall return to this point in my conclusion).

In light of this extrinsic definition, the public use of history likewise figures in works conceived of and executed as scientific works and which nonetheless have a public impact beyond the scope of a circle of scholars. I refer to such works, to cite two Italian examples with very different significations, of the biography of Mussolini by De Felice and Pavone's book on the Resistance.[2] Professional historians are not exempted either; they make public use of history when they speak of mass media; this is evident in the case of the *Historikerstreit*, in the German "dispute among historians" with regard to Nazism.[3]

Before going any further and assessing the solidity of a definition so vast and yet so fragile, I would like to present a few reflections on the difference between this initial definition and the definition adopted by Jürgen Habermas during the dispute among historians.[4] Habermas likewise initially chooses an extrinsic definition (by distinguishing clearly for example between that which is written in scholarly contexts and that which is conveyed by mass media), but he makes it more rigid with an opposition of principle. Making public use of history is anyone who "speaks in the first person" and proposes explicit politico-pedagogic objectives: establishing a consensus around a few fundamental values for civilian coexistence.

Habermas thus in effect presents an opposition between public use of history and scientific activity which, in the terms he uses to support it, is not convincing. On the one hand he develops in a coherent fashion the lesson of the Frankfurt school, which is inspired by a mistrust of the manipulation always lurking in matters of mass culture: "The critical public is supplanted," he writes in his *History and Critique of Public Opinion*, by the manipulating dimension."[5] And he adds that the progress apparently brought about by the blossoming of public debates is contradicted by its reduction to a simple consumer commodity. On the other hand he proposes an idea of scientific and more specifically historical activity as a conscious choice of the "third person," characterized by a distance taken from the object under examination and the control of one's prejudices and personal predilections. I shall return to the second problem later on, in my third point. For the moment I shall limit myself to the observation that in Habermas' argument the specificity and the enormity of the problem of Nazism for a German assumes a decisive weight; whence arises the invitation to historians to respect, for therapeutic and political reasons, the *prius* (primacy) of the moral condemnation and the uniqueness of Nazism when discussing the mass media, reserving for the domain of scientific research the more relative comparisons and the balances of responsibility (both topics broached, as we know, by Eric Nolte with respect to Bolshevism).[6] This position is debatable when it comes to method, even if it may be shared with regard to the polemic against Nolte himself.[7]

As concerns the mass media, Habermas' detailed critical examination often attains its goal, but in my opinion it is reductive. The enlargement of the domain of the public use of history proposed here implies in effect that it is not identified as a political use in the strictest sense and even less as political manipulation. There are also, in mass media and elsewhere, manifestations of the public use of history that have no explicit intention but simply offer diversion or escape; and there are finally uses of the past which directly implicate individual or collective memory and which have in my opinion an entirely different significance and liberating potential.

In short, the public use of history is not a practice to be rejected or demonized on principle; it may be a ground for comparison and conflict involving the active participation of citizens, and not only scholars, on essential topics. It can reveal profound tears and memory wounds and bring them to light. It can on the other hand be a form of manipulation which establishes misleading analogies and crushes the present with the depths and complexity of the past.

Momentarily leaving aside the latter phenomena and those leading to a purely passive use of the past—which nonetheless probably make up the predominant tendency—I would like to limit myself to citing a few examples of the public use of history which have had a particular impact on the political and cultural life of Western societies—as points of comparison and conflict and, at the same time, instruments for the growth of the collective consciousness.

I am thinking of the emergence of Jewish memory and the French "repression" of Vichy, as shown in the fine study by Henry Rousso.[8] The turning point in the perception of events as if from a great distance, and in the dissolution of repression, is tied to the debate elicited by Marcel Ophüls' film *Le Chagrin et la pitié* and then stoked by the trials of former collaborators. The role that the media can play in such cases is immense: at times this is intended, as in this particular case, with perhaps some unforeseen effects; at times unforeseen and unintended, as was the case in Germany with the television airing of *Holocaust*, a mediocre production which was nonetheless capable of provoking questions and examinations of conscience in a vast public.

I am thinking of the phenomena of "public history" in the United States, as least in as much as it calls into question the processes of the triggering and construction of memory: for example, in situations of advanced deindustrialization, the reflection on industrial heritage; or on another level, and with consequences which are not always happy, the research into ethnic memories as instruments for the construction of an individual or collective identity.[9]

I'm thinking, finally, of the Italian debate on Fascism and antifascism, in which the repercussions are obvious in the political sphere and in the so-called transition to the "Second Republic."[10]

In short, this brief list is merely intended to underscore that it is opportune, when treating thematics at the frontier between historical research and the construction of public opinion, to proceed with care and humility, especially for those for whom history is a profession, in research or teaching.

It might be helpful to bring up a situation which accentuates the urgency for a reflection on the relationship between history and the public use of history for historians, and represents it as a sort of professional duty. Such a reflection, indeed, has been made more current by the ruptures and upheavals of the last few years, which have marked the end of the century—a diagnosis which has now become almost commonplace: from the fall of Communism to the Gulf war, from the civil war in the former Yugoslavia, to the crisis and the profound transformation of the Italian political system. In opening the newspaper or turning on the television, one encounters airy, superficial interpretations, often falsely iconoclastic, of the recent past, even if more serious reflections and accurate readings are not lacking. In both cases it becomes clear that the periods in which the public use of history becomes most demanding and intrusive correspond to phases of sudden transformation or profound historical discontinuity which change the very way we situate the present in relationship to the past. One might then say—leaving aside the distinctions between and the distancing from the most instrumental forms of the public use of history—that we are dealing with, in a certain sense, physiological phenomena (and as I shall attempt to do in points 1) and 2), one should question oneself on the novelty, from this perspective, of the situation in which we live.)

For this same reason I find insufficient and erroneous the widespread tendency among professional historians to feverishly hunt down the current practices of rewriting the past in order to expose them and disparage the results. Before denouncing or exorcising the contents of such practices, one must analyze how they are concretely activated, and which stereotypes or unintended yet at the same time symptomatic mechanisms are put into play. Moreover a purely reproachful attitude and the mere activity of correcting errors and distortions with a blue pencil, however justified, will certainly never succeed in stemming or directing into the channels of philology the extremely rich flow of direct or indirect communications on history (called the "system of history"),[11] which cannot but escape the control of the guild of historians.

We are dealing with a task which calls for the recruiting of many people, and many have been recruited already: far from pretending to offer a serious panorama in the very rich domain of the public use of history, I shall limit myself here to exploring the relationship between the history of historians and the public use of history.

1. History and the Public Use of History: Contaminations and Conflicts

In making these introductory observations, I have already broached the topic. To confront it is far from simple because, in addition to the obvious oppositions which, as we have seen, absorbed the attentions of Habermas and hundreds of others with him, and to which we shall return, there also exist strong elements of contamination, interrelations, proximity or at the very least reciprocal influence. I shall thus proceed schematically, by points and successive approximations, without any pretense to exhaustiveness.

Meanwhile I must point out that, if we peruse the history of Western historiography, history and the public use of history do not become literally distinguishable from each other until recent times; they used to be one and the same thing.

I will not and cannot elaborate here; but we must stress the fact that the public use of history is its own justification, in as much as it is an activity which governs and defines the relationships between memory and oblivion, between what is worthy of being retained and what is not; and, in the definition of these relationships, the dominant weight is entrusted to the guardianship of the community, in other words to politics. Thucydides asserts that the object of his reflections is the Peloponnesian War, since he does not think that the events which preceded it, in the most ancient times, "are very important either in terms of war or in terms of other issues."[12] The history he tells is the history of the Greeks, as different and superior to the others, the Barbarians. The model of the Peloponnesian War, furthermore, must be eternally valid since, given the immutability of human nature, past or future events can never transpire in the same way.

Thus, in Thucydides and in all of Greek historiography, the emphasis is placed on the idea of development, continuity; this was equally a distinctive characteristic of Jewish thought, then of Christian thought, before becoming the patrimony of the historicism of the twentieth century. Continuity and development mean that the past makes us what we are in the here and now; it is the root of the importance that political power has always given to the control of the past as a privileged instrument for the control of the present.

The political function of historiography is to regulate memory and oblivion in order to shape the characteristics and the collective identity of a community and to distinguish it from others; and to construct, thanks to the past, a project and a prophesy for the future. Such are the visible and never completely abandoned connotations, as we see, of the historiographic enterprise up until recent times; and these are, at the same time, the strong elements of what precisely distinguishes the public use of history.

In the article on history he wrote for the Einaudi Encyclopedia, Jacques Le Goff illustrated the course of historiography in the light of these same parameters, placing particular emphasis on the connection to politics. He brought up, for example, how in Renaissance Italy there emerged a historiography aimed at celebrating the past glories of the cities and how, in Venice, with the annals of Andrea Dandolo in the middle of the fourteenth century, we find what one could call, according to a symptomatic definition, the "pubblica storiografia" or "storiografia comandata" (public history or commanded history). In the France of Louis XIV, one sees the flowering of court historiography, drawn up, and here again the definition is symptomatic, by the "king's historians."[13]

There is, however, another element which distinguishes the historiographic enterprise and makes its scientific pretensions valid: the demands for freedom and criticism in its research. Indeed, one finds this explicitly articulated in the first pages of Thucydides work. In *Le radici classiche della storiografia moderna*, a posthumous work which appeared in 1993, Arnaldo Momigliano concludes a rich and complex analysis with a lapidary judgment: "If modern historiography is a critical product, it is Greek and not Jewish"— and not Christian one might add, for this is clear from other passages of the work.[14] And yet modern historiography, which begins with Spinoza and is developed in the nineteenth century, the historical century, is not only a critical product; as Momigliano himself is quite aware, historiography is also the fruit of a continual "tension," regularly put into question and eternally unresolved, which is the reason for the fascination as well as the damnation it arouses, a tension "between history, the future and prophesy."[15] It is a scientific activity *sui generis*, whose cognitive dimension touches and mingles with the affective dimension, which is steeped in values, predilections, and non scientific or pre-scientific choices.[16]

The difficulty encountered by historians in developing a strong scientific status: the use of a natural language which does not provide for, as in other disciplines, the passage of a threshold requiring special training; or, inversely, the difficulty of introducing to the general public works adopting more complex techniques and methodologies—not to mention the objective importance of its regulation for the functioning of society itself: it is perhaps for all these reasons that the domain of history is open to all types of inroads. It's as if one admitted, to adapt a famous phrase, that history is too important to be left to historians.

2. Twentieth-century Innovations

In general terms, there is thus a close yet conflictual relationship between historiography and the public use of history. To explore and eventually unravel this tangle, it is thus necessary to delve deeper and then propose a few hypotheses of division by period. One hears repeated on all sides, especially on the left, that it is precisely in the present time that the practice of the public use of history is the most continuous and the most invasive, and that its processes of revision are the most arbitrary. In his reflection on Togliatti and Communism, Gianpasquale Santomassimo, for example, has observed that at least in Italy, in keeping with a typical reversal with regard to the public use of history after the war, today people no longer seek a legitimization of present choices in the past. People legitimize—or rather annul—the past itself to respond to immediate political objectives.[17]

On the opposite side, Sergio Romano, referring to the way Germans and people from the Balkan countries talk of the mass graves of Katyn and the German-Russian pact of 1939, writes that "this is not historiography, but a no-man's land where the past is only used if it serves to influence the present."[18]

And one could cite other examples, beginning with the quagmire of the Second World War and the gross revisionism of which it has been the object these past years: this goes from the work of the German author who considers the conflict as a simple episode in the Soviet strategy aiming to control the world, to the recent essay by a French historian who defines the partisans, including Jean Moulin, as agents of the Soviet secret services, to new attempts to deny the extermination of the Jews.[19]

Should we therefore conclude that today we live in an exceptional period in terms of the public use of history?

The answer is rather ambiguous: not only because the manipulation of history and its use as an instrument have known otherwise somber moments during the course of the twentieth century,[20] but because today there arises, in a guise still which remains inexplicable, a paradox whose origins date far back. The paradox lies in the fact that two apparently contradictory phenomena coexist today: on the one hand an accentuated and widespread eradication of the past, a total "bringing into the present," so to speak and, on the other hand, a hypertrophy of historical references in public speech.

The premises of this eradication, tied in an obvious way to the processes of modernization, are situated, especially in Europe, at the true beginning of the twentieth century, at the time of the First World War: after its end, in the twenties and thirties, the relationship between history—understood here as *res gestae*—and the public use of history came to a decisive turning point. In essence there was an almost perfect temporal coincidence between this profound rupture and especially *the perception of it* by millions of Western men and women, and the appearance of technical conditions permitting the development of the means of mass communication. A grandiose work of modernization, occurring in the particular circumstances of a war of unheard-of proportions, and profoundly marked by them, set about settling accounts with history in a dramatic and radically new way; moreover, the emergence of the means of mass communication offered a powerful and new vehicle for its broad diffusion.

Nicola Chiaromonte has described with exemplary clarity and not without emotion the effects of this historical turning point: "Why was it," he writes, "that the Socialist movement, which had undoubtedly constituted the most vigorous and intellectually rich attempt to promote the cause of justice and equality in Europe, was so overwhelmed by the explosion of the First World War that it never succeeded in reconstituting itself in a politically efficacious and ideologically convincing fashion?"[21] Along with Socialism, Chiaromonte adds, other equally solid beliefs also lost their way: "The legitimacy of the appointed order, the supremacy of the will to reason, faith in change." And he concludes: "How was an idea defeated by an event?" This question is simple only in appearance, and its echo comes down to our own time, which has known the defeat of a similarly large idea.

The event, that which has already taken place, thus dominates men and women and does not permit a return to the past. As Chiaromonte observes once again, "there is nothing more durable, in the world of men, than a common belief as to the nature of things; but its duration has no other guarantee than the exterior of the state of things that are reflected in it and which itself is subject to the order of time. One turn of history's wheel—one event—suffices to destroy it, and when it is destroyed, no will to belief suffices to restore it."[22]

There ensues a refusal of history, and thus nihilism; but also an openness to allow oneself to be captured by new promises on the part of anyone capable of setting in motion a sort of historical short-circuit. Thus it is no accident that Fascism/Nazism and Communism are so attractive to certain kinds of historicism: the former manipulates modernity by decking it out in the reassuring cloak of tradition, while the latter demonstrates a much more complex attitude toward the past. Communist historicism, indeed, combines the refusal of history and the beginning of a new history: it claims to have the inevitable course of history on its side, but at the same time it fights for the forgetting of the preceding history of human oppression because this is the condition for constructing a utopia—which seemed in fact on the verge of becoming reality after the success of the October revolution.

But the dominant feeling in the postwar years remained anxiety, the uncertainty between abandon and refusal, a constant ambiguity. Perhaps no one has expressed this ambiguity so adroitly as the English poet W.H. Auden, who writes, "Madonna of silences to whom we turn/ when we have lost control": this is addressed to history, to its silences, to all that is hidden behind its silences, the search for comfort, appeasement, self-pity. But it is a search whose results are far from certain; there is an enigma behind these silences, an end of the security of a linear, meaningful course of history. The questions addressed to Clio remain unanswered; but one can say "yes, like a lover," and thereby give in to her unpredictable course: "Your silence already is there/ between us and any magical center/ where things are taken in hand."

And historiography also makes a contribution to the closing of the circle, with the crisis of classic historicism in the Western democracies, and especially the now complete rupture with the figure of the nineteenth century historian, uncontested master of the public use of history, now challenged and pressured by the historiography produced by the mass media.

This is why the current situation does not seem at all new. If the public use of history assumes such flashy ways today, it is because history has changed again (as we said, the century is ended), and because, in certain ways, historiography has changed as well.

3. Conflicts

We can now return to the opposition between history and the public use of history according to the terms defined by Habermas: the public use of history would adopt the first person, historiography would instead express itself in the third person. I have already briefly alluded to the fact that historiography is not only a cognitive enterprise, but likewise an affective one, even if one of its ethical qualities, so to speak, is the control exerted on its own predilections and personal values; and even if, on the other hand, the rule every historian worthy of the name submits to, the guarantee of the scientific character of his work, is the philologically unassailable use of the sources he uses. But the differences can certainly not be overestimated: and they lie not only in the method, but above all in the criteria of selection of subjects and sources.

This is where the conflictual relationship between memory and history comes to the forefront. The selectivity of historiography lies within the logic of the discipline: it is precisely for this reason that nothing is foreign to the historian's eye. Collective memory and group memory, which is precisely that which sets into motion a large part of the public use of history and which is in turn influenced by it, works on the contrary alongside the obligatory and exclusive paths defined by unforeseen and discontinuous individual or collective emergencies. The opposition between collective memory and history is exactly the result of the process which led the historian to separate himself from the "organic life of the people," in refusing to transform memory into history, as they claimed to do in the nineteenth century.[23]

The theme of individual and collective memory would require an in-depth study, especially with regard the selection processes of the past, and thus its relationship to oblivion and its contradictory ties to politics.[24] Suffice it here to say that such memory has dual value: the reclaiming or redemption of a hidden or denied past, and the opaque expression of the distance of the past. As Michael Frisch writes, memory can effectively create a distance from the past in a paradoxical manner, because it interprets it by the light of the present and thereby crushes it: this is the context of the contemporaneity which attacks the structure of memory, if history does not come to its rescue and put the past into perspective and place it back into context.[25] A recent and heated polemic between two Jewish historians referring to the history of the extermination has however further complicated the terms of comparison: each maintains, for opposite reasons, the opposition between history and memory, and their conclusions raise important doubts concerning the advisability of conceiving of this relationship in dichotomous terms.[26]

As for its relationship to politics, memory again plays an ambiguous role. In classical Greece, as Nicole Loraux has shown, politics begins where the memory of the past, with its atrocities and its divisions, ends: for the good of the community, it is advisable for the past to pass on, that the conflicts between citizens be erased and oblivion triumph (this is the problem raised today by the German revisionists); whereas the refusal to allow the past to disappear activates a critical memory and fosters a different politics, which elaborates a mourning based on this past.[27] As Agnes Heller writes, "one can only authentically forget what is first authentically remembered."

To return to the historians, I present two quotes. The first is by Paul Veyne: "Historians define history as the social function of historical memories and situate them as belonging to an ideal of truth in the pure interest of curiosity."[28] The second is by Piero Bevilacqua, who asserts that among historians, even among those who were the last to follow this course, the Italians, "the bond between ethics and knowledge has been broken."[29] These two converging quotes, which describe a process which has actually taken place in the international historiography of this second postwar period, together suggest a plan.

Our two colleagues are certainly correct if they wish to indicate the obsolescence of the figure of the historian as unique interpreter and sole builder of collective and national identities.

But their plan does not meet with the consent of all historians: one might even argue that there exists a relationship which is not fortu-

itous between the recent developments in research and the intensifi-
cation of the public use of history. One need only look at how themes
considered used-up, outmoded and henceforth impossible to propose, and which seem uniquely reserved for the public use of history,
are becoming central to the work of historians: the themes of the
nation-state, national and ethnic identity, cultures and collectively
shared thought processes; and, above all, the way in which these subjects are all broached with a pedagogic and prescriptive intent. This
reversion, which at times is presented in a neohistoricist guise, at
times with more scholarly or more sophisticated instruments, such as
deconstructivism or "weak thought," can be explained in a number
of different, if not alternative ways. These tendencies can be read: a)
as the simple result of the *historical* developments in progress, which
show the reemergence of movements having a national or ethnic
base and of fundamentalisms of different sorts; b) as the simple
reflection of a restoration on cultural grounds; c) as the rediscovery of
traditional themes, after the attempt at "scientization" and parcelli-
zation of the historical domain (with the transformation of historiographical work into an esoteric enterprise or one more or less
reserved to a restricted number of experts); d) as a symptom of fail-
ure, erosion, or refusal or at least the non-exhaustivity of analytic categories which define different types of belonging, first and foremost
the category of "class"; e) and finally as the tormented arrival of the
social history of a culturalist or oralist stamp (of particular relevance
in this regard is the case of the German *Alltagsgeschichte*, some of
whose representatives, in studying Nazism, have taken refuge in the
consoling rediscovery of the *Heimat*). It is shocking in any case to find
in the essay of a sophisticated aficionado of post-structuralism, the
American historian David Harlan, an unconditional approval of a
phrase of Richard Rorty, the most extreme of extremist "historicists":
that history should become an enterprise which is "more therapeutic
than reconstructive, more edifying than systematic."[30]

4. The Politics of History

We shall now broach the problem of communication strategies
and symbols particular to the public use of history, and especially

the public use of history directly or indirectly governed by political power. Herein, inversely, lies the greatest distance between the practices implemented and a historiography worthy of the name, but we should not be surprised to see historians appear among the divulgers. As is in fact the rule in the mass media, one finds men and women at the center of these stories, people who are preferably exceptional for one reason or another, or at the very least known by everyone: never or hardly ever does one find structures or contexts.

What seems particularity interesting to me is the relationship of many of these practices to legal procedures: figures from the past are asked a riddle and judged at "history's tribunal." I'm thinking particularity of the practice of "rehabilitations," a practice most useless for those directly concerned, those condemned and often physically eliminated, yet nonetheless fundamental for the holders of power because, in a solemn form and with a great symbolic impact, they convey a strong message to the public. Rehabilitation is, in appearance, a particular case of that rewriting of history which, as stated by a well-known proverb, is the task of each new generation. But in fact it corresponds to a demand for legitimization of determined systems of government and indicates the defeat of the group or regime which inflicted the original condemnation. Furthermore, it illustrates a parallel to the practices of penal justice, in the form of judicial error. And the protagonists here are not historians or intellectuals in general, who function more like the Napoleonic code or as simple executors. The examples are many and multiple and do not only concern totalitarian societies, which are the most skilful at stirring them up. One need think only of the rehabilitation of Bukharin by the Gorbatchev's USSR. Does not the announcement made by the poet Yevtushenko of his intention to dedicate a poem to the most famous victim of the Moscow trials elicit some irony, or worse?

Rehabilitations can also be limited to indicating a change in *policy* of the institution which implements them, a change which necessarily involves a complete rupture with the past. I'm thinking of the rehabilitations which arose after the destalinization in the USSR in the nineteen-fifties, and especially in the Western Communist parties, which were administered as much by the groups in power as by the past. Or of rehabilitations that are impossible by law, given the working mechanisms of the specific institutions, but which indeed took place (such as the way in which the Catholic Church revised the condemnation of Galileo).

In these supervised games of rewriting the past, the practice of reevaluation accompanies that of rehabilitation. It concerns figures who did not undergo formal condemnations from the judicial or political powers but who, for cultural or ideological reasons, were foreign to the foreseeable horizon of the dominant orthodoxy and are later paradoxically recuperated to illustrate or confirm specific political objectives and organize a consensus around a system, political movement or an ideal. We may recall the reevaluation of the image of Frederick II of Prussia in the former East Germany, or that of Peter the Great in Stalinist Russia, where the objective was to organize a consensus for these respective regimes. Or again to the *encomiastico* judgment pronounced by the secretary of the Italian Communist party, Palmiro Togliatti, on Giovanni Giolitti, in relation to the political polemic resulting from his confrontation with Alcide De Gasperi.[31] In truth, reevaluation serves as a bridge with the work of historians and also sheds light on differences of strategy and objectives. Carlo Ginzburg extracts from the past, and in this sense "reevaluates," a sixteenth-century miller condemned by the Inquisition: not, however, to exculpate him from the accusation of heresy, but to support a specific interpretation, in this case that of the circularity of culture.[32]

5. Conclusions

Because of its open and provisional nature, this essay does not require formal conclusions. I shall therefore refer to two very different examples, which are situated at the two ends of the spectrum of the *feedback* that the public use of history elicits on contemporary society, in order to confirm the problematic and contradictory character of this field of study.

"While in the recent past men and women died 'for their country,'—after 1945 they said that my grandfather also died 'for his country,' in Theresienstadt—in this *fin de siècle* they die, and they kill, for memory's sake."[33] This is a bitter judgment, which can be applied, among other cases, to the use of memory by the national or ethnic identities in former Communist societies, in particular in former Yugoslavia where "invented traditions" functioned and function still as the cutting tools of ethnic conflicts coldly conceived and stirred up. Here we can measure the strategic importance and the tragic effects of the public use of history.

At the other extreme we find a case of the debate over the national past, one which grew out of all proportion in Italy between 1989 and 1993, during the crisis of a political system that had emerged after World War II. It is a crisis that presented itself as a pure and simple disintegration and transmitted these characteristic features to the manner in which history is used. In Italy, the paradox—already marked by a violent eradication of the past, in the forms described by Lanaro,[34] as well as by a hypertrophy of historical references in public speech—does not seem to be enough to activate the collective historical consciousness to build a consensus—and perhaps does not even wish to do so.

History is used above all as an instrument of the day-to-day political battle: but it is a dialogue that takes place strictly within the ruling political class. History does not appear here as the construction site of great coherent and ideological narratives or at least as constructions of meaning. It is more a pool in which people fish for more or less fortuitous examples, useful for the latest polemics. The object is no longer to educate a people but to reach an audience, through history but not only, with the spectacle of politics.

All the more reason why, then, is it necessary for the public use of history to be conscientious and critical, capable of questioning the opacity and the eternity of the past to redeem it from the tyranny of the present.

Translated by Sophie Hawkes

Notes

1. This article is a revised version of a paper given at a conference on "L'uso pubblico della storia," held in Rome in March 1993 and organized by the Istituto romano per la storia d'Italia dal fascismo alla resistenza. The proceedings are in press and will be published by Franco Angeli, Milan.

2. R. de Felice, *Mussolini*, vols. 1–4 (6 vols.), (Turin, 1965–1990) and C. Pavone, *Una guerra civile. Saggio storico sulla moralità della Resistenza* (Turin, 1991). It is at any rate clear that the impact on the public of R. de Felice's historiographic hypotheses is more due to the criticisms(such as *Intervista sul fascismo*, ed. by M. Ledeen [Bari, 1975]) or the numerous interventions of a more direct political nature in the daily press or periodicals or on television during the last twenty years than to the weighty tomes of the Duce's biography.

3. I am referring to the Italian collection of this debate: G. E. Rusconi (ed.), *Germania: un passato* che non passa. I crimini nazisti e l'identità tedesca, (Turin, 1987).

4. See Habermas's criticism, ibid.

5. J. Habermas, *Storia e critica dell'opinione pubblica* (Bari, 1988), 213; published in English as *The Structural Transformation of the Public Sphere* (Cambridge, Mass., 1989).

6. Apart from his interventions in the *Historikerstreit*, cf. his work *Marxism, Fascism, Cold War* (Assen, 1982).

7. I have discussed Nolte's positions in N. Gallerano, "Storia, memoria, identità nazionale," in: *Passato e presente*, 20–21 (May-December 1989), 219–231.

8. H. Rousso, *Le Syndrome de Vichy. De 1944 à nos jours* (Paris, 1990) (Orig. publ. 1987).

9. M. Frisch, *A Shared Authority. Essays on the Craft and Meaning of Oral and Public History* (New York, 1990).

10. N. Gallerano, "Critica e crisi del paradigma antifascista," in: Idem (ed.), *Fascismo e antifascismo negli anni della repubblica*, Problemi del socialismo, n.s. VII (1986), 106–133; idem, *La memoria pubblica del fascismo e del antifascismo*, in: AA.VV., *Politiche della memoria* (Rome, 1993), 7–20.

11. P. Ortoleva, "Storia e mass media," in the conference proceedings quoted in n.1 above.

12. Thucydides, *Histoire de la guerre du Péloponnèse*, I, 1 (Paris, 1966), 31.

13. J. Le Goff, *Storia*, Encyclopedia Einaudi, vol. XIII (Turin, 1981).

14. A. Momigliano, *Le radici classiche della storiografia moderna* (Florence, 1993).

15. Cf. the analysis of Momigliano's book in A.I.Iacono (ed.), *La talpa libri*, 5 February 1993.

16. Boddei,"Addio al passato: memoria storica, oblio e identità collettiva," in: *Il Mulino*, XLI, 2 (1992), 179–191.

17. G. Santomassimo, "Tradizione comunista e azzeramento della storia," in: *Passato e presente*, n.s. IX, 22 (1990), 9–18.

18. S. Romano, "Gli usi della storia,", in: *Il Mulino*, XLI, No.2 (1992), 207.

19. I am referring to E. Topitsch, *Stalin's War: A Radical New Theory of the Origins of the Second World War*; T. Wolton, *Le grand recrutement* (Paris, 1993). As regards the "negationists," it suffices to refer to the works of P. Faurisson, recently—and unwisely—legitimated in parts at least by E. Nolte.

20. M. Ferretti has given an excellent description of the annulment of the historical memory in the USSR during the Stalinist era in *La memoria mutilata. La Russia recorda* (Milan, 1993).

21. N. Chiaromonte, "Credere e non credere," in: *Il Mulino* (1993), 116.

22. Ibid., 118.

23. Y. Yerushalmi, "Réflexions sur l'oubli," in: AA.VV. *Usages de l'oubli* (Paris, 1988).

24. P. Di Cori, "L'oblio, la storia e la politica. A proposito di alcuni recenti pubblicazione sulla memoria," in: *Movimento operaio e socialista*, 3 (1990), 297–316.

Nicola Gallerano

25. Cf. M. Frisch, op.cit., 12.
26. A. J. Mayer, "Memory and History: On the Poverty of Remembering and Forgetting the Judeocide," in: *Radical History Review*, 56 (1993), 5–20; O. Bartov, "Intellectuals on Auschwitz. Memory, History and Truth, History and Memory," in: *Studies in Representation of the Past*, V, 1 (1993), 87–119. I have commented on this controversy in "Memoria e storia: un dibattito", in: *Passato e presente*, XII, 33 (1994), 105–111.
27. N. Loraux, "Sur l'amnistie et son contraire,", in: AA.VV. *Usages de l'oubli*, op. cit.
28. P. Veyne, in: Le Goff, *Storia*, op. cit.
29. P. Bevilacqua, "Sull'uso pubblico della storia," an account of the intervention in the debate on the subject, in: *Annale 1991* (Rome, 1992).
30. D. Harlan, "Intellectual History and the Return of Literature,", in: *American Historical Review*, 3 (1989), 604. The quotation by Rorty is from his book *Philosophy and the Mirror of Nature* (Princeton, N.J., 1980), 5.
31. P. Togliatti, *Discorso su Giolitti,"* in: *Momenti della storia d'Italia* (Rome, 1963), 79–116 (but the text dates from 1950).
32. C. Ginzburg, *The Cheese and the Worms* (Baltimore, 1979). Subsequently Ginzburg has returned several times to the convergence and the difference between historians and judges with regard to the problem of evidence; cf., i.a., *Il giudice e lo storico* (Turin, 1993); "Just One Witness," in: S. Friedlander, *Probing the Limits of Representation. Nazism and the Final Solution* (London and Cambridge, Mass, 1992).
33. A. Mayer, op.cit.
34. S. Lanaro, *Storia dell'Italia repubblicana. Dalla fine della guerra agli anni novanta* (Venice, 1992), in particular the reference to the "great transformation of the 'sixties", 223ff.

Notes on the Contributors

François Bédarida has taught at the Sorbonne, the Institut d'études politiques de Paris, the Ecole nationale d'administration. From 1978 to 1991 he served as founding director of the Institut d'histoire du temps présent. His current position is that of directeur de recherche at C.N.R.S. His recent publications include *La Société anglaise du milieu du XIXe siècle a nos jours* (1990), *Lettres de Marc Bloch a son fils* (1991), *Le Régime de Vichy et les Français* (1992) and *La France des années noires* (1993).

Enrico Florescano studied history at the Colegio de México and at the Sorbonne. He was i.a. director of the National Institute of Anthropology and History of Mexico. His works include *Precios del maiz y crisis agricolas en México, 1707-1810* (1986), *El nuevo pasado méxicano* (1991) and *Memoria méxicana* (1994).

Nicola Gallerano teaches the history of contemporary Italy at the University of Siena and is president of the Roman Institute for the History of Italy from Fascism to Resistance (I.R.S.I.F.A.R.) as well as co-editor of *Passato e presente* and *I viaggi di Erodoto* and a member of the academic advisory board of *Ventesimo secolo*.

Aaron I. Gurevich was born and educated in Moscow. He held professorships at the universities of Kaliningrad, at the Institute of Philosophy and, finally, the Institute of General History at the Russian Academy of Sciences. He has published numerous works on culture, including *The Raids of the Vikings* (1966), *Categories of Medieval Culture* (1972), *Medieval Popular Culture: Problems of Belief and Perception* (1988), *Medieval World: Culture of the Silent Majority* (1990).

Eric J. Hobsbawm was born in Alexandria. He taught i.a. at King's College, Cambridge; Cornell University; the New School for Social Research. Among his best known publications are *Primitive Rebels (1959)*, *The Age of Revolution* (1962), *The Age of Capital* (1975), *Nations and Nationalisms since 1780* (1990) and *The Jazz Scene* (1993).

Christian Meier was born in Pomerania and studied at the universities of Rostock, Göttingen and Heidelberg. He received his PhD from the University of Frankfurt in 1963. He held professorships in Ancient History at the universities of Basle, Cologne, Bochum and, since 1981, at the University of Munich. His publications include *Introduction à l'anthropologie politique de l'antiquité classique*, (1984), *Vierzig Jahre nach Auschwitz* (1987,1990), *Kannten die Griechen die Demokratie? Die Nation, die Keine Sein Will* (1991), and *Athen. Ein Neubeginn der Weltgeschichte* (1993).

Paul Ricœur studied at the University of Rennes and the Sorbonne. He taught as Professor of the History of Philosophy at the University of Strasbourg, Professor of Philosophy at the Sorbonne and Nanterre and at the University of Chicago. He is the author of *Temps et Récit* and *Soi-meme comme un autre* etc.

WOMEN, FAMILY and SOCIETY IN MEDIEVAL EUROPE
Historical Essays, 1978–1991

David Herlihy

Edited by Anthony Molho

Until his untimely death in February 1991, David Herlihy, Professor of History at Brown University, Rhode Island, was one of the most prolific and best known American historians of the Middle Ages. The author of books on the history of thirteenth- and fourteenth-century Italy, Herlihy published, in 1978, his best known work in collaboration with Christiane Klapisch-Zuber, *Les Toscans et leurs familles* (translated into English in 1985, and Italian in 1988). For the last dozen or so years of his life, he launched a series of ambitious projects, on the history of women and the family, and on the collective behavior of social groups in medieval Europe.

This volume contains most of the essays which he wrote after 1978. They convey a sense of the enormous intellectual energy and great erudition which characterized David Herlihy's scholarly career. They also chart a remarkable historian's intellectual trajectory, as he searched for new and better ways of asking a set of simple and basic questions about the history of the family, the institution within which the vast majority of Europeans spent so much of their lives.

Contents: Introduction by A. Molho—My Life in the Profession—Women and the Sources of Medieval History: The Town of Northern Italy—Did Women have a Renaissance?—The Natural History of Medieval Women—Women's Work in the Towns of Traditional Europe—Making Sense of Incest: Women and the Marriage Rules of the Early Middle Ages—Family—The Making of the Medieval Family: Symmetry, Structure, Sentiment—The Family and Religious Ideologies in Medieval Europe—Santa Caterina and San Bernadino: Their Teachings on the Family—The Florentine Merchant Family in the Middle Ages—Medieval Children—Biology and History: Suggestions for a Dialogue—Age, Property and Career in Medieval Society—The Problem of the "Return to the Land" in Tuscan Economic History of the Fourteenth and Fifteenth Centuries—Florence's Economic Relations with its Subject Cities in the Fifteenth Century—Tuscan Names, 1200-1530—The Rulers of Florence, 1282-1530—Appendix: The American Medievalist.

Anthony Molho is Munro Goodwin Wilkinson Professor of European History at Brown University, Rhode Island, and has written several works on the social, political, and economic history of late medieval and early modern Italy.

April 1995
ca. 400 pages
ISBN 1-57181-023-4 hardback
$59.95/£45.00
ISBN 1-57181-024-2 paperback
$17.95/£11.95

Berghahn Books
165 Taber Avenue
Providence, RI 02906   USA
401-861-9330

FRANCE AND AMERICA
IN THE REVOLUTIONARY ERA
The Life of Jacques-Donatien Leray de Chaumont, 1725–1803

Thomas J. Schaeper

This is the first detailed account of the life and career of Chaumont whose chief claim to fame was the fact that from 1777 to 1785 Benjamin Franklin lived in his home in the Parisian suburb of Passy. Basing his work on documents from two dozen archives in the United States and France, Schaeper demonstrates that Chaumont was far more than merely a landlord. Prior to the American Revolution he had become one of the most powerful and respected businessmen of the Old Regime. For personal as well as patriotic reasons he aided the American insurgents and worked with a wide array of persons. In addition to Franklin, these included John Adams, Silas Deane, Caron de Beaumarchais, the marquis de Lafayette and the comte de Vergennes. Chaumont performed an astounding range of services—acting as an intermediary, an adviser, and a supplier of arms and clothing. His most dramatic contribution to the American cause involved John Paul Jones. It was Chaumont who obtained the famous *Bonhomme Richard* for the commodore. Through looking at the activities of this intriguing individual the author is able to offer many new insights into both American and French history. Lively and well written this biography will appeal both to the historian and the general reader.

Contents: Chaumont's First Fifty Years—France and the Coming of the American Revolution—Chaumont enters the Picture—Benjamin Franklin's Landlord and Friend—Other Americans in Paris—Congressional Supplies—Private Trade with America—John Paul Jones: Friend—John Paul Jones: Enemy—Financial Ruin—Twilight Years—Appendix: Eighteenth-Century Currencies

"... very well researched...excellent coverage of the pertinent materials...there is simply nothing that compares with it in American or French literature....the definitive account on Chaumont." **William Stinchcombe**

Berghahn Books
165 Taber Avenue
Providence, RI 02906 USA
401-861-9330

April 1995
ca. 400 pages
appendix, 7 half-tones, 1 map, bibliog., index
ISBN 1-57181-050-1 hardback
ca. **$59.95/£43.00**

JAPAN AND GERMANY IN THE MODERN WORLD

Bernd Martin

With the founding of their respective national states, the Meiji Empire in 1869 and the German Reich in 1871, Japan and Germany entered world politics. Since then both countries have developed in strikingly similar ways: The Japanese, after experimenting with American, English and French models of modernization, finally opted for the Prusso-German example which they followed from 1881 to 1945, when they restructured not only the Meiji constitution but also the entire administration, the modern legal system, the education system from the village school to the Imperial University, the Imperial Army and last but not least the social system. It is not surprising therefore that these two countries became close allies during the Second World War, although in the end it proved a "fatal attraction." The developments in both countries since the war have again shown remarkable similarities. Yet this fascinating parallelism has been largely neglected in Western scholarship. This volume by one of Germany's leading Japan specialists will fill this gap.

Contents: The Prussian Expedition for the Far East—Fatal Affinities: the German Role in the Modernization of Japan in the Early Meiji Period (1868–1895) and its Aftermath—The Politics of Expansion of the Japanese Empire: Neo-Imperialism or Pan-Asiatic Mission?—Japan during the World Economic Crisis: Big Business and Social Unrest—The End of the Old Order: Social Change in Japan during the Pacific War—Three Forms of Fascism: Japan—Italy—Germany—Germany between China and Japan: Germany's Far Eastern Policy of the Interwar Period—Japan and Germany on the Path towards War: Mutual Influences and Dependencies — Germany and Pearl Harbor—The German Japanese Alliance in the Second World War—The Pacific War and Twentieth Century—Select Bibliography—Index

Bernd Martin is Professor of Modern History at the University of Freiburg/Br. Although he is well known for his work on Japan, his interests extend to the history of modern Southeast Asia, and he frequently lectures, in addition to Japan, in China, Taiwan, South Korea and Thailand. He has published numerous book and articles on modern Germany and Southeast Asia.

Berghahn Books
165 Taber Avenue
Providence, RI 02906   USA
401-861-9330

May 1995
ca. 256 pages
ISBN 1-57181-858-8   hardback
ca. **$39.95/£28.00**

THE HISTORY OF THE ARMENIAN GENOCIDE
Ethnic Conflict from the Balkans to Anatolia to the Caucasus

Vahakn Dadrian

The Armenian genocide, though not given such prominent treatment as the Jewish Holocaust which it preceded, still haunts the Western world and has assumed a new significance in the light of "ethnic cleansing" in Bosnia. This study by the most distinguished scholar of the Armenian tragedy offers an authoritative analysis by presenting it as a case study of genocide and by seeing it as a historical process in which a domestic conflict escalated and was finally consumed by a global war. It also establishes a link between genocide and nationality conflicts in the Balkan peninsula and the Turko-Armenian areas. The author furthermore looks at the six Great Powers of Europe, who played an important role in these conflicts and critically examines the idea of "humanitarian intervention" under which they operated. He finally deals with the international legal aspects of the Armenian genocide as "crimes against humanity," a principle formally adopted for the first time by the Allies in May 1915, under the impact of the Armenian genocide, and compares it with the trials in Leipzig in 1921–22 and those of Nuremberg after 1945. This volume contains the results of twenty-years of research and analysis and will no doubt be considered the definitive work on the subject for some time to come.

From the Contents: Humanitarian Intervention by the Powers: A Historical Perspective—The Rudiments of the Turko-Armenian Conflict—The Dysfunctions of Humanitarian Intervention in the Rise and Treatment of the Armenian Question—The Inauguration of a Proto-Genocidal Policy of Annihilation—The Wars and Massacres of the New Young Turk Regime and the Demise of Humanitarian Intervention—The Initiation and Consummation of the Genocide under Cover of the First World War—The Quest for Justice in the Aftermath of Turkish Military Defeat—The Push beyond Domestic Genocide: The Targeting of the Russian Armenians—A Review of the Armenian Genocide in a Comparative Perspective—Conclusion—Appendix: The Pool of Potential Sources in Nazi Germany Regarding the Facts of the Armenian Genocide.

About the author's work: "... an outstanding work of scholarship ... based on years of meticulous study of primary sources ..."   **Leo Kuper, University of California**

"... the author [...] pioneered the sociological study of the Armenian genocide ..." **Roger Smith, College of William & Mary, Virginia**

Vahakn N. Dadrian received his PhD from the University of Chicago and was Professor of Sociology at the State University of New York, Geneso. He is currently director of a large genocide study project supported by the H.F. Guggenheim Foundation.

Berghahn Books
165 Taber Avenue
Providence, RI 02906   USA
401-861-9330

July 1995
ca. 500 pages
ISBN 1-57181-016-1 hardback
ca. $65.00/£45.00